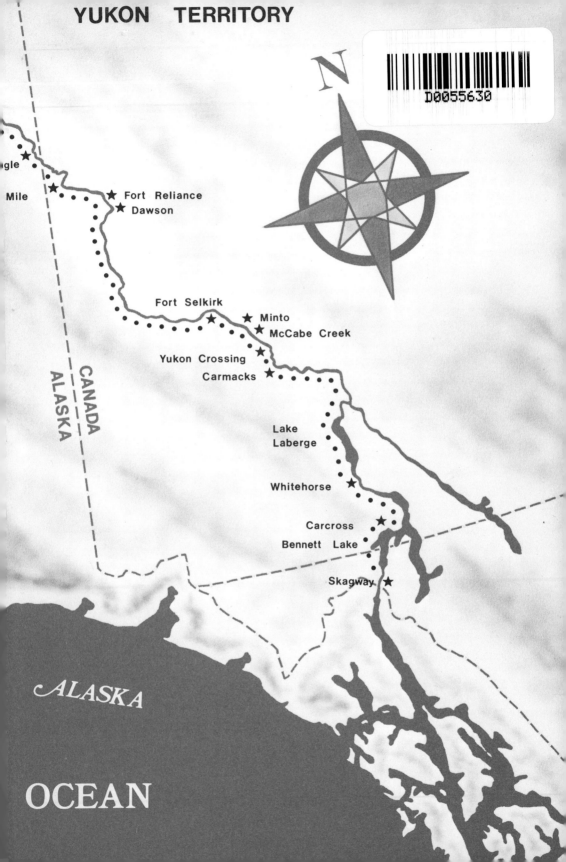

YUKON SUMMER

YUKON SUMMER

BY EUGENE CANTIN

CHRONICLE BOOKS

To N.T. and A.M.
Who made it all possible.

With thanks to Rich Haupt for the title "Yukon Summer."

1st Edition

Library of Congress Catalog Card Number: 73-84519
ISBN No. O-87701-043-9

Published by Chronicle Books
54 Mint Street
San Francisco, California 94103

Contents

Introduction

The first book that I can remember ever having read is *The Bounty Trilogy*, by Nordhoff and Hall. Perhaps it is because of the influence of this early fare in literature, with its desperate men working their way to distant and exotic destinations, that much of what I have read and found enjoyable over the years has followed a similar vein. I've explored dark forests with Conrad, poured tacks out onto my decks with Slocum to ward off curious natives, sailed to distant ports with Chichester, Heyerdahl, and Melville, and clambered up great mountains with Ullman, with Herzog, with Tilman and Mirkle. I found these men and their exploits absolutely marvelous, and like anyone else who reads such works, I could not help but wonder what it would be like to actually indulge in such adventures.

But always I was a "dreamer by night":

> All men dream: but not equally. Those who dream by night in the dusty recesses of their minds wake in the day to find that it was vanity: but the dreamers of the day are dangerous men, for they may act their dream with open eyes, to make it possible. This I did—T. E. Lawrence.

Of course, Lawrence was a very dangerous man indeed, for his waking dream was of war and the making of an Arab nation. But the distinction he expresses is a valid one, even for less war-like men. My dreams, always "by night," had been of some sort of extended confrontation with nature, in which I would be forced to trust myself to myself. It would be worthwhile and even fun, I thought, to somehow travel under my own power through lands which I did not know, seeing if I could prove equal to whatever challenges and experiences might come my way. For years these thoughts remained with me in one form or another, but I never attempted to make them come true, to become one with the "dreamers of the day." Then on June 7, 1972, I put a small one-man kayak into Bennett Lake, in British Columbia, and the sort of adventure I was used to reading about in books began to unfold about me.

The Yukon River is the fifth longest on the North American continent. It rises in a 75-mile chain of five lakes—Lindeman,

Bennett, Nares, Tagish and Marsh—that curve north out of the mountains in the upper corner of British Columbia. From these five lakes the river flows on a northwest course for over 500 miles through Canada's Yukon Territory. Then it enters Alaska and continues on its northwest route to a point just above the Arctic Circle, where it turns in a southwesterly direction, running for a total of roughly 1,500 miles through Alaska before finally emptying into the Bering Sea. The Yukon is a very large river indeed.

I did not go the length of the river, nor did I establish any kind of speed record over the portion that I did cover. And I certainly cannot claim any sort of "first ever" record as a traveler on the river: Since the early days of the Klondike gold rush, probably 50,000 men have traveled over part or all of the Yukon. There were, however, at least three "firsts" for me on this trip: It was the first time I ever saw any part of this beautiful and historic waterway. It was my first view of white water from a boat. And it was the first kayak trip of more than an hour or two that I had ever undertaken. (A few hours on the "fearsome" lake waters of Berkeley's Aquatic Park and Livermore's Del Val reservoir, and short stretches on two of California's more placid rivers, were the extent of my experience.)

In the months leading up to June 7, when I put my kayak into the ice-bound waters of Bennett Lake in British Columbia, I developed a number of beliefs—all singularly unconnected with reality—about the Yukon and what traveling down it might be like. The days between June 7 and July 8, when I pulled my kayak out at Tanana, Alaska, 1,200 miles downstream, were largely given over to a program of personal education conducted by the river, during which my initial opinions came to agree rather more closely with the river's reality.

For extremely well-written and very enjoyable background material on the history of the Yukon, I recommend two books: Richard Matthew's *The Yukon* and Pierre Berton's *The Klondike Fever*. Both make fascinating reading, and I am largely indebted to these two works for my small knowledge of the history of the region I traveled through. Of course, any mistakes in presenting that history are my responsibility.

Eugene Cantin
Berkeley, California

Incantations

There is no more fatal blunderer than he who consumes the greater part of his life getting a living.—Henry Thoreau

If a man does not keep pace with his companions, perhaps it is because he hears a different drummer. Let him pace to the music which he hears, however measured or far away.—Henry Thoreau

What does a man need—really need? A few pounds of food each day, heat and shelter, six feet to lie down in—and· some form of working activity that will yield a sense of accomplishment. That's all—in the material sense. And we know it. But we are brainwashed by our economic system until we end up in a tomb beneath a pyramid of time payments, mortgages, preposterous gadgetry, playthings that divert our attention from the sheer idiocy of the charade—Sterling Hayden, *Wanderer*

I wanted to get me a full pack complete with everything necessary to sleep, shelter, eat, cook, in fact a regular kitchen and bedroom right on my back, and go off somewhere and find perfect solitude and look into the perfect emptiness of my mind and be completely neutral from any and all ideas. I intended to pray, too, as my only activity, pray for all living creatures; I saw it was the only decent activity left in the world.—Jack Kerouac, *Dharma Bums*

To be precious, the heritage of wilderness must be open only to those who can earn it again for themselves.—Garrett Hardin

I wondered how far I should turn out faithful to that ideal conception of one's own personality every man sets up for himself secretly.—Joseph Conrad, *The Secret Sharer*

You can't get to a pleasant place to be at unless you use pleasant methods to get there.—Clarence Darrow, *Clarence Darrow for the Defence*

You have many years to live—do things you will be proud to remember when you are old.—John Brunner, *Stand on Zanzibar*

1   A Dreamer of the Day

If I am to explain how my kayak voyage down the Yukon came about, I must introduce you to a friend of mine, Steve Jacobson. Steve, like so many of my friends, seems a typical child of our times—a person of many excellent talents who seems unable to find a really functional place for them in our hectic world. Steve went through the University of California at Berkeley, picking up a B.A. and, I believe, a Phi Beta Kappa key, then went on to get an M.A. in math. Of course, there were no jobs available for a person with such a degree; so, for a while, Steve turned his considerable attention to leather craft, training himself to make excellent belts and sandals. I've worn one of his belts for the past three years, and shall probably wear it the rest of my life.

Off and on, as Steve ground his way through or was ground up by school, he would disappear for a few weeks or a month or a year. He had discovered Alaska. He first went north during a summer vacation, on a car-camping expedition up the Alaska Highway. Next, he spent a year in our largest state, working for Vista in the Eskimo village of Marshall at the foot of the Yukon. In the winter of 1971, Steve was back in Berkeley attending Cal again, but he was still thinking about Alaska. He announced that he was planning to take a kayak trip down the Yukon River.

I have always loved maps, maps of any sort, and I think I first began to be caught up in thoughts of going to Alaska myself when Steve, sitting in his tiny apartment in Albany, spread out his 250,000:1 topo maps of the Yukon River. We began to work our way down the river inch by inch, and all along its length wondrous names appeared, such as Lake LaBerge, Fort Selkirk, Moosehide, Forty Mile, Purgatory, Deadman Island, and Moosehead Rack. What would it be like up there? What sort of people lived alongside the river? What do these colored lines and squiggles on Steve's maps really say about the realities they represent? I didn't know it then, but I was hooked.

Steve's next move was to acquire a used Klepper Arius, a kayak made with beautiful Germanic ingenuity to come apart and fold up into two relatively small canvas carrying bags. Early one morning I found myself accompanying Steve to Berkeley's Aquatic Park to help him with his maiden voyage. We found the park nicely deserted and drenched in early morning sunlight, the park's small lake barely rippling in the wind kicked up by the cars passing on the Bayshore Freeway just to the west beyond a screen of trees.

Steve went straight to work. Out of the two canvas sacks he pulled a pile of neatly made sections of wood and a hull of canvas and rubber. Steve fitted this rod into that socket, these brackets into those slots, slid the resulting light wooden frames into the canvas and rubber hull, and after 20 minutes of effort my friend was paddling about in a personal yacht 2 feet wide and some 15 feet in length. The kayak rode in the water like some lean and mythic sea creature. It was downright exciting.

Steve paddled around a bit, then allowed me to give it a try. The most difficult and nerve-wracking part of this my first excursion in a kayak was simply getting into the boat. Steve is small and slight; I am neither. My knees hit the coaming before I was safely seated, and I nearly went over with the ship. At that point I discovered that Steve has one terrible failing—he doesn't know when it is an appropriate time not to laugh his head off.

Once I was underway on the waters of Aquatic Park, I felt so insecure that I didn't dare turn even my head for fear such a wild gyration might instantly tip my silly craft straight over. So I paddled about sitting as still as I possibly could, looking like an Egyptian mummy come partially to life. But it was kind of fun, sliding absolutely silently along on the water, trusting a thin hull of rubber to keep me afloat and dry. Maybe a person really could set out in one of these things and seriously expect to survive.

Steve set off for Alaska a few weeks later, his ancient but seemingly indestructable Rambler loaded down with equipment. As the summer progressed, I received outrageously uninformative letters from Steve about the progress of his trip from Fairbanks to Marshall, down the lower portion of the Yukon. "Trip going well, head winds bothersome. Lost a map. Steve." would be about typical. He managed to complete the trip and, to my surprise, stayed on in Alaska afterwards. He is still there, married now to a lovely Eskimo girl, Anna, who makes delicious *akutaq*, an Eskimo ice cream made of berries, shortening, sugar and seal oil.

I spent the months after Steve's departure going about my business, which is mainly teaching tennis, with a bit of photography and article writing on the side. One October day I happened into the Ski Hut, one of Berkeley's great camping and hiking stores, and found myself looking over the newer editions of the intricate

Klepper Arius. I was only looking, you understand, nothing more; but one of the salesmen happened to mention that the price of the kayaks was due to go up because of a recent devaluation of U.S. currency. He added that it took some time to get the boats shipped in from New York and that only a phone call could guarantee one before the cost went up. Before I could fully consider what I was about, I had put in an order for $396.87 worth of kayak, spray cover, rudder and assorted other items. I mean, after all, look at all the money I was saving. I still wasn't thinking about taking a trip in such a boat, of course; but, really, shouldn't everyone have a folding kayak around, just in case?

Several times that winter I took the kayak out for practice sessions, going to Aquatic Park, to the Del Val reservoir behind Livermore and to the smooth valley rivers that run through or by Modesto. No white water, no real speed, nothing that might really test the abilities of a rank beginner. But it was fun putting the boat together, hopping in (actually, more of a careful crawl than a hop), and paddling off along some quiet waterway which might reveal almost anything from quiet glades and deer to trailer parks and garbage dumps. I even tipped the boat over several times, in a small lake managed by a friend in the Sierra foothills. I wanted to see if I could master the Eskimo Roll, the trick by which you right yourself after going over, with a neat little squiggle of your paddle and an adroit maneuver of your hips. I determined conclusively that my talents ran to the *half* Eskimo Roll, and no further.

I find that I have a strange way of setting about any sort of ambitious or unusual project. I seem to find it necessary to sneak up on the project a step at a time, stoutly denying my intentions all the while and even ridiculing the very idea of whatever it is I am secretly setting out to do. Thus, as spring came to the Bay Area, I sent off for maps of the Yukon—"just to see what the river looks like"—and slowly began to collect this item and that of equipment "in case I ever might want to make some kind of river trip someday." I went into a travel agency "because it's raining outside" and just happened to learn the cost of the air fare to Juneau and a return from Fairbanks. And I sent Steve letter after letter, asking naive questions about his trip down the river—"What do you mean, 'cache your food'? Are there bears on the river?" I am quite sure that those friends who received the brunt of my speeches on the absurdity of such a trip, the total foolishness of anyone like myself even thinking of undertaking a solo kayak trip down the Yukon, knew long before I did that I was going to give such a trip a try.

Sometime during the spring I came across the perfect name for my Klepper Arius: "*Quisnam igitur sanus?*"—a question from Horace which translates roughly as "Who, then, *is* sane?" By now I was beginning to consciously, actively admit that I was thinking about trying a trip down the Yukon. And what could be a better title than this for the craft of someone who had no real experience in a kayak, had only a vague (and largely mistaken) idea about what the Yukon River might be like, had never been anywhere near Alaska before, and really ought to stay home and earn a living? So, of course, I finally decided that I really had better go down the Yukon and see what it was all about. After all, "*Quisnam igitur sanus?*"

Toward the beginning of May, my preparations swung into high gear. These consisted largely of sitting for long hours trying to imagine what sorts of equipment I would need for this or that facet of the trip, then wandering in and out of stores looking for the equipment. In planning and purchasing equipment I found myself thinking in terms of systems: a sleeping system (two-man tent, down sleeping bag, foam and ensolite pads); eating system (white-gas stove, alternate grill, water bottles, pots and utensils, food bag, cookhole in the tent, waterproof matches); photographic system (a typewriter case filled with two Nikon bodies, four lenses, various filters, lenshoods and shades, a changing bag, a tripod, and great quantities of black and white and color film); location and communication system (two dozen 250,000:1 topo maps covering the entire river, two compasses, a map measurer, a large legal tablet in a hard-cover folder, and a number of pens); clothing system (rubber boots, leather hiking boots, tennis shoes, net underwear, a pullover shirt, two sweatshirts, a down parka, rain pants and parka, two mosquito headnets, a hat, dark glasses, and an extra pair of prescription glasses); health system (vitamins, adhesive and bandages, tweezers, antiseptic cream for minor repairs, lots of mosquito repellent, suntan lotion and dry skin cream, toothpaste and soap); and an entertainment system (several paperback books, a tiny tape-recorder for recording any interesting conversations I might encounter, and, of course, the entire kayak and its equipment, which were to afford me the entertainment of traveling down the Yukon). To my great surprise and joy, I found, once I was enroute, that my equipment planning and purchasing had been virtually perfect. I used every bit of equipment that I had along, even the tape recorder; yet I found no real need for any additional items. The one exception was the damned stove, which never worked when I most needed it.

During this period of preparation I finally began to admit to friends and acquaintances what they already were taking for granted: that I was planning to take a kayak down the Yukon. Almost without exception, the ensuing conversation would go something like:

"The Yukon? Where's that?"

"It starts in Canada and runs through Alaska to the Bering Sea."

"Who are you going with?"

"No one."

"You're kidding. You *can't* go alone."

"Oh, well, there are people along the river. And if anything happened to the boat I could just hop in the river and drift down to the next settlement anyway."

"What about the *bears*?"

Always it seemed to come down to this: "What about the bears?" People who do not go out into the countryside a great deal know with unshakeable certainty that there is *something* out there which "goes bump in the night," and for lack of a better bugaboo they give it the title "bear." Since I am one of those very people who do not get away from the city all that often, and as more and more of my friends asked me what caliber bazooka I was planning to carry in order to protect myself from those slavering beasts, I began to half believe their fears. Those bears were surely going to come from hundreds of miles around to devour me and perhaps my beautiful kayak as well. Under the impact of all this, I went out and purchased three road flares. I might get swallowed, but the swallower was certainly going to get a burned throat as I went down. These preparations and concerns turned out to be purely academic; I didn't see a single bear while on the Yukon.

My confidence was shaken again when all my dear friends thought it would be a good idea for me to read James Dickey's *Deliverance*, which deals with the sodomy, murder and shipwreck four men encounter on a canoe trip. I made the mistake of reading the book.

Even before reading *Deliverance* I did have several areas of doubt about the trip in my own mind. In large part, all of these worries were formless—merely the typical diffuse apprehensions that seem to infect most people facing a new enterprise. And, in fact, one reason I was interested in this trip was precisely to overcome this sort of self-constructed hurdle once again. It seems to me that the more times you push aside your reluctance to do something new and then find the new experience enjoyable, the easier it becomes to do so the next time and the next.

I also had a few specific and very real worries. For one thing, I would be carrying roughly 150 pounds of boat and equipment. How everything came to weigh that much I do not know. The boat weighed only 50 pounds, and the rest of my equipment just couldn't have amounted to an additional 100 pounds, although in fact it did. I wondered how in the world I would be able to carry such a mass of stuff through the transportation systems—plane to Seattle, plane to Juneau, ferry to Skagway, train to Bennett Lake—to my destination. And I tried to think as little as possible about how all of this equipment was going to fit into my tiny kayak.

Another concern involved the problems I might have with officials or citizens and other travelers along the river. The wilderness and the animals in it are both impersonal and disinterested. If one is alert and well-prepared, he really shouldn't have any problems. But people are the great variables. One of my worries, for example, was whether or not the Canadian Mounties, with whom you are supposed to check in while on the river, would let such a kayaking novice as myself out into their wilderness. Two other travelers whom I met on the river were incredibly prepared for their expedition—"incredible" is the only term that does justice to their mass of equipment for every contingency—but they had had great difficulty talking their way past a border official hundreds of miles away from the river to the south. He doubted the adequacy of their preparations. I'm very glad that I didn't meet him or any other official until I had been on the river for several days. As for the few residents and my fellow adventurers along the Yukon, I had no serious problems. One great benefit of the trip was learning all over again how people are pretty much the same wherever you meet them, and how rare it is to find someone actively malevolent toward you, especially in the wilderness where people are so dependent upon one another.

The actual travel on the lakes and rivers of the Yukon seemed the least of my worries. I am a fairly confident swimmer and am not afraid of the water. If I went over, I planned to slip out of the kayak, swim to shore with the craft and its carefully lashed and wrapped equipment, dry off and put on some dry clothing from a waterproof carrying bag, then get into my sleeping bag until I was warm. No problem. Occasionally the thought did occur to me that if I was somehow to lose the whole boat, I might be in some difficulty. But proper attention to detail, I thought, such as carefully tying up the boat at each landing, would ward off that possibility. A lost paddle would be a pain, but I intended to carry a spare, using it as the base for some of the baggage I hoped to anchor on the kayak's rear deck. Fortunately, I did not ask any experienced kayaker about the wisdom of putting baggage in a great mound there. I'm sure they would have blanched so badly at the thought of so unbalancing a kayak that my enthusiasm for the trip might never have recovered.

Despite all my lingering concerns, I really was committed to the trip and was waiting impatiently for the day of departure. And I had made up my mind to travel alone, despite bears and *Deliverance*. For one thing, who else could I find who would want to make such a crazy trip? And for another, I had discovered from earlier camping trips the joys of being able to get up when you want, stop when you decide to, and eat when and what you care to, without reference to anyone else. Also, I have the feeling that when you are with another person, much of your attention is concerned with that person, rather than with the new world that surrounds you. And, finally, when traveling with a companion, you can't present yourself as yourself to whomever you meet along the way. Instead, you become a unit of two individuals, which is quite a different proposition. I also must admit that I thought I would rather encounter the inevitable difficulties of the journey on my own rather than under the observation of a quite probably more experienced fellow traveler. This trip was to be very much a learning process for me, and I felt that I could learn more on my own.

On Sunday, June 4, that learning process began. I entered San Francisco Airport, accompanied by 150 bulky pounds of equipment and my strange, inaccurate ideas of what lay before me. I boarded a 727 bound for Seattle and a connecting flight to Juneau, then wedged myself, my camera case and a shoulder bag into seat 12A, economy section. Fortunately, the airlines hadn't begun their routine of luggage searches, or I would probably never have made it onto the plane with my hunting knife and the flares that looked dangerously like sticks of dynamite. On the other hand, the headlines—"Skyjack Thwarted: Skyjacker Planned Water Escape with Kayak"—would have given me subject matter for another kind of book.

The jet slanted across the bay and over the Berkeley Hills into a clear blue sky. Within a few minutes I had settled back into the seat and into that timeless, encapsulated feeling one always has on a plane. I did quite a bit of mental wandering in the course of my enforced reverie; when a look out the window reveals so many of man's pretensions reduced to an ant world, you cannot help but slip into musing and doubts and second thoughts about your own grand plans. What exactly was I about, I wondered? As the miles streamed by, I found a number of answers, a few of which I will list here: I was making the trip because I believed that I could gain from challenging the new and unknown and conquering my apprehensions in the face of such a challenge; because so many people I know, myself included, often find themselves out of joint with the life in our cities and towns and need to "come home" to the empty lands to refresh themselves; because I wanted to confront nature on an extended basis, to see what it is like to live away from "necessities" and "comforts" not just for days but for weeks; because I was curious about the Yukon, about its history and what it has become today; because the journey seemed to promise a great deal of fun; because I've discovered that I am more awake and alive when I'm traveling, that I can clearly recall each day's activities on trips taken five years ago, whereas what I did last week in the normal daily routine is usually a mystery; because I wanted to be among "the dreamers of the day" to the limited degree that it was possible for me; and, finally, because when I wasn't trembling before this or that phantom fear, I thought the whole idea seemed glorious.

2   Arrival at Bennett Lake: Bennett Station

On any good map of the upper Yukon, Bennett Lake appears as a very narrow, 25-mile length of blue running almost due north from the eastern base of the Pacific Boundary Range of mountains. It is the second of the five lakes—Lindeman, Bennett, Nares, Tagish and Marsh—that stretch in a long question-mark curve from the mountains toward Whitehorse in the Yukon Territory. The map also indicates that the White Pass Railroad runs from Skagway over the 2,900-foot White Pass summit and then down to a station at the head of Bennett Lake. But maps at best are only very limited symbols for reality. They tell you nothing about how you will feel as the White Pass train carries you from Skagway up over the pass, twisting and turning up the sides of the gorges, carrying you from spring back into a winterland of snow and ice and very cold air.

The White Pass Railroad is one of the few still-functioning remnants of the Klondike gold rush. In 1898, tens of thousands of men, goaded by the lure of easy riches, struggled over the extremely rugged Chilkoot Pass to reach the upper lakes of the Yukon, lugging with them the 2,000 pounds of supplies that the Canadian Mounties insisted they carry. A longer rival route—the White Pass—was opened by businessmen in Skagway, who hoped to wrest much of the lucrative trade with the would-be miners from the budding town of Dyea below the Chilkoot Pass. Because the White Pass route involved a more gradual climb on which pack-horses could be used to speed the movement of cargo, the town very quickly became a roaring boomtown. The trail was a great success for everyone except the beasts of burden who toiled on it. According to one account, at least 3,000 of the Skagway pack-horses died working on the trail, and their bodies were often left where they dropped, to be ground to pulp by the endless lines of men and horses passing over them. Finally, the stench of carrion grew so horrible with the coming of spring that the citizens of Skagway came out onto the trail to clear it of carcasses, lest the smell make their route unpopular.

Eventually Skagway passed under the control of the notorious Soapy Smith and his gang, who turned the town into an evil con show, preying mercilessly on the miners who passed through. Those miners who were aware of what was going on must have breathed a sigh of relief when they crossed the passes and entered the calm, efficient domain of the scrupulously honest Canadian Mounties.

The White Pass Railroad, a nearly impossible engineering problem, was begun in May of 1898 and began serving the miners, businessmen and hustlers of Skagway and Whitehorse in 1900. Today the railroad carries tourists and containerized cargo into the Yukon area, as well as moving great loads of ore to a mammoth shipping dock on the Skagway waterfront. As I rode along in an old-fashioned passenger car, sweating in the oppressive heat from a glowing oil-burning stove in one corner, I found it very hard to imagine the passing forests filled with the sounds of thousands of men clambering and cursing their way over the cold and rugged passes to the headwaters of the Yukon and the goldfields beyond. But I did my best to recreate the scene in order to pass the time and distract my mind from my concern over the wintery landscape outside my window. In Skagway several people had expressed doubts that Bennett Lake would be sufficiently clear of ice to navigate, and everyone warned me of the dangerous winds which could pile up enormous boat-swamping waves along the length of the lake when it was clear. And now I could see for myself that a small lake on the summit was completely iced over and that the clouds swirling about promised more snow to come. Bennett lay 20 miles further north but several hundred feet lower in elevation. I could only hope that the weather would be better down there.

As the train descended the snowy forested hills toward Bennett, I turned from one window to another, searching for a first glimpse of my destination. All the tension and excitement of several months of casual and not so casual preparation were condensed into these last few minutes. I found my emotional state switching back and forth from near exaltation at finally reaching the end of the journey and the beginning of the adventure to nervous trepidation at what I might find at Bennett. There was only a moment's view of Bennett Lake before we took the last plunge down toward the station, but that was long enough for me to think that I saw a band of ice stretching across the lake. I couldn't be sure, and within a few minutes I was much too busy getting myself and my equipment off the train to give it any further thought.

The White Pass Railroad station at the head of Bennett Lake consists of a long wooden platform fronting the tracks, backed

Skagway's main street, looking toward Halutu Ridge.

by a large dining hall and several peripheral buildings to house the cooks and waitresses who work there. Each day the trains from Skagway and Whitehorse meet at Bennett, and everyone scrambles out, is hastily fed a large family-style meal, then hustled back onto the trains for the remainder of their journey. For 30 minutes or so around noon each day there is frantic activity about the station, then both trains pull away and even the station employees seem to disappear, returning the upper end of Bennett Lake to its empty silence.

When the train came to a halt and I climbed down from the car to stand in the cold air on the Bennett platform, I made a wonderful discovery. Standing there, with the train huffing and puffing beside me, a scant hundred yards from the lapping headwaters of the Yukon, all my cavilling thoughts slid away and I could feel exciting reality pluck me up. The wooden platform of the station, the sand between the tracks, and the water of Bennett Lake were all perfectly real. Whatever was going to happen to me on the Yukon could begin to happen now, and I found myself welcoming—joyously—this change of condition.

As the other passengers on my train disembarked and hurried to the dining hall, I went to the baggage car and unloaded my equipment, putting it in a neat stack in a corner of the station wall near the dining room entrance. As I worked, I was very conscious of being observed with interest—or perhaps it was disbelief—by both the train crew and the passengers. They would look at me and my baggage, realize that I was leaving the train here at Bennett, then survey the empty cold country that surrounded us and the dark clouds scudding along overhead. Most of them shook their heads slightly before proceeding inside to eat; and when I joined them in the dining room, I found that I already felt separated and apart from my fellow passengers of just a few minutes before.

With a momentary laughing thought of being the condemned man eating a last meal, I wolfed down the beef, potatoes and bread which were passed up and down the long tables. The meal was quickly finished, and the crowd of well over 100 tourists pushed back out through the doors and onto the trains. I left the table with them, then fidgeted about with my pile of canvas bags and boxes, trying to look busy for all the curious eyes watching me but really just waiting for them all to go away.

At last the trains huffed into action and chugged down the tracks in opposite directions. A few drops of rain fell from the sky, and for long minutes I simply stood on the station platform, looking about. The silence, after the noise of the trains and people, was uncanny, and the pure, biting air felt very good and welcome, both against my skin and in my lungs. Mountain air—clean, crisp, with that hint of pine scent in it—has always seemed to me the proper stuff for men to breathe, and here I found no exception.

Immediately ahead of me, as I looked out from where I stood under the wooden eves of the station, sand flats stretched under a sparse covering of long wild grass to the beach at the head of the lake. A hill stood beyond the tracks to my left, overlooking the lake, and at the top of the hill there were several wooden buildings and a log church, its steeple rising tall among the second-growth pines. Beyond the church I could see the massive, snow-covered slopes of the Boundary Ranges, which keep the headwaters of the Yukon from flowing the 25 miles to the Pacific and instead force the river to begin its 2,000 mile journey to the Bering Sea. The narrow blue-green lake stretched off to my right for three or four miles, where a slight curve of the stark surrounding mountain walls cut off my view. Overhead, grey-black cloud roiled, hiding the cliff-tops which hemmed the lake.

Although Bennett Lake lies only about 2,100 feet above sea level and the surrounding snow-sloped mountains reach only 7,000 feet, the area seemed much higher to me, and as rugged and beautiful as any I have seen in the Sierra, Europe or Nepal. The combination of sheer mountain wall, blue-green water and slate-grey clouds overhead was magnificent. Probably it was I who was high with excitement and anticipation, and I simply carried my surroundings along with me.

At last I walked across the tracks and down the sandy slope toward the lake, looking for a good campsite. A grassy portion of the sand near the base of the hill looked promising, but when I got there I was exposed to an increasingly stiff and chilling wind, which made the site considerably less appealing. I walked to the water's edge, the wind tugging at my clothing, and for the first time I became aware of hearing the most startling and lovely sound —the notes of chimes, delicate and beautiful wind chimes, filling the air. I was entranced—and puzzled. Where was it coming from? And then I realized that the sound was being made by thousands of pencil-sized shards of ice floating in a narrow band on the current flowing from the outlet of Lindeman Lake. The shards were jostled by the wind and current on Bennett so that they clinked gently together and filled the air with the unexpected music. I thought this symphony of nature a fine and beautiful welcome. I didn't know it then, but within 24 hours I was going to hate that sound.

I walked back to the station platform and began carrying my equipment away from the strangely artificial silence of the station to the natural silence of the sand flats near the lake. On my second trip back to the station, two men began hammering nails on an addition which was going up, but somehow the very human sound of hammering only increased the isolation and deserted feeling of the station. I walked over to one of the men, a great bear of an Indian, and asked him about the line of ice I thought I had seen on the lake from the train.

"There's ice there, all right," he said, "but it's just rotten. You can push a boat right through it." He looked carefully at me. "Where are you going?"

"Down the river," I answered as casually and vaguely as possible.

Real concern showed in the man's eyes. "Your boat better be good—these lakes can really get rough. Three, four foot waves down at the other end of this one, and they'll kick up in a moment. Stay out of the middle, and really take it careful." He went on to suggest that I stay in one of the log cabins on the hill by the church. "There was a guy here just before you; he's been waiting for the ice for a couple of weeks now. He stayed up there."

I thanked him, and returned to the sand flats with my things. I took another long look at the lake. Three or four foot waves, hmmm? Well, we'd just have to see.

Wondering about my predecessor and whether or not he had managed to "push right through" the ice and was cruising happily at the far end of the lake, I walked up the hill to the cabins to look them over. But I found them littered with junk and broken glass. The log church, however, was large and airy and seemed quite comfortable and inviting despite its dirt floor. The logs were heavily carved with names and dates, and an aged plaque on the outside of the church announced its founding and founders:

> *This church was built in 1899 under the auspices of the Pres-*
> *byterian Church of Canada. Dr. Jason Robertson was then*
> *superintendent of missions, and Rev. J. A. Sinclair was the minis-*
> *ter in charge. At that time thousands of men were encamped*
> *here building boats for the journey to the Klondyke.*

Thousands of men—and now the church stood here alone, abandoned as it has been for decades. This was one facet of the Yukon that had fascinated me as soon as I began to read about it: how very crowded and feverish this upper end of the Yukon had been during the gold rush, and how empty it is today. And now, standing there, I had only to turn on my heel and look around to see silent pine forests where 10,000 men had once worked madly to throw together insane contraptions they optimistically called boats for their futile race down the lakes and the river to the gold fields. In all of the North American continent there must be only a few such places, where men have come in great numbers and then left again in a few short years, never to return.

I moved my 150 pounds of belongings for the third time that day and spread them out comfortably in the door of the church. Then when a gap appeared in the clouds and the sun pushed forcefully through them, I unpacked my camera and several lenses and climbed up the hill behind the church. I wanted to take some photos of my departure point, and I also hoped that the 300mm telephoto lens might be able to tell me more about the ice on the lake.

A few minutes walk through the trees and up several sheets of sloping rock brought me to the crest of the small hill. The only sounds about me were the distant tiny hammering sounds of the workmen down at the station and the rustle of the wind pushing pine needles about. Bennett Station, surprisingly small and isolated against the surrounding mountains, was directly below me; and to my left, beyond where Lake Lindeman lay hidden in the trees, I could see a diagonal slash in the snow running down from a shallow pass on the crest of the Boundary Ranges. I decided that this had to be the route of the Chilkoot Trail, and I couldn't help wondering what it must have been like for men to slog down those slopes during the frigid winter months, after the incredible effort they expended carrying their kit up the steep Pacific side of the trail. Even as I stood there, in June, the air seemed crisp and wintery through four layers of shirts and sweatshirts.

I took a number of pictures of the Chilkoot Pass and of the old log church with the blue-green ribbon of the lake in the background. Then I put the long lens on the camera and looked off toward the white line of "rotten" ice stretching across the lake. The narrow white line was actually a rather broad expanse of ice, which seemed to cover the lake from side to side for at least a mile or two. Its surface seemed to be broken in many places, with open patches of blue water showing through here and there. The workman's judgment was apparently correct. I should be able to simply paddle through the floating ice and continue on down the lake.

I went back down toward the church, enjoying the warmth of the late-afternoon sun and the good feelings of being back in the mountains. I even toyed with the idea of getting the kayak together and setting out to cover a few miles in the remaining daylight hours, but I soon put that thought aside. The kayak would take a long time to load, especially since I had never tried packing all of my equipment into it. I also suspected that I needed a long evening's sleep more than I realized, that the energy I was now feeling was mostly due to excitement. Just carrying the equipment about in Skagway and here at Bennett Lake had proved a fair day's labor.

When I reached the church, I discovered what every hiker seems to have to learn the hard way, each time out: Food left in the open attracts hungry visitors. A gnawed apple and a missing raisin boxtop announced that I had unwittingly been holding open house; and within a few minutes, my guest, a bold tree squirrel, was sneaking across the church floor for another sample. I suggested that he look elsewhere for his evening meal, then settled down to mine: cracker under butter under jam topped with blue cheese. Scrumptious!—and yes, I may as well admit at this early point that I am blessed with a very high tolerance for ordinary, even questionable food. I find myself quite happy eating meals which most of my friends find appalling. A full stomach of any sort, with a vitamin pill tossed in on top to ward off the possible inroads of scurvy, seems to do the job for me. On my way down the Yukon I planned to get my food from stores in the villages along the way, and the satisfying fare I devoured in the church above Bennett Lake, purchased in a market in Skagway, suggests the practicality of my plan: I was easily pleased, and anything a tiny village store had to offer was certain to keep me happy and full.

After eating I read for a bit, then spread my tarp on the ground just inside the doorway of the church, lay the ensolite pad and foam mat on top of that, and put the sleeping bag and myself on top of the mat. It was about 11 p.m. by this time, but the room was still dimly lit by the far north sun which never really seems to set. It was clear that I would have little need for the flashlight and extra batteries I was carrying. I had hung my food bag from a roof support, and when I had settled down to sleep, my uninvited guest—or was I his uninvited guest?—returned to work his way all around the ceiling supports trying to get to the bag. He finally gave up the futile effort, and I went to sleep listening to the silence, if you can accept such a paradox, and hoping for clear weather for tomorrow's start down the Yukon.

The Anglican Church at the head of Bennett Lake.

3   Ice and Company

My journal entry for the next day, June 7, begins "A day of education, and even adventure." The education came on many levels as the elements of my surroundings pushed and pulled and tore at my preconceptions about the river, until by the end of the day, these beliefs came to line up a bit more closely with reality. It was a grey morning, and I had a little trouble motivating myself into activity, even though it was the day for the beginning of an experience I had been thinking about for months. I ate a leisurely breakfast and wandered around the church for a while, until I got my mind and body awake. Then I spread the tarp on the sandy soil in front of the church and laid all the boat pieces on it. It took only about 20 minutes to piece the hull frames together, slide them into the hull, and blow up the air tubes which form the kayak's gunwales. It took nearly twice that long to lash the spare paddle and my pack frame to the rear of the boat with lengths of nylon clothesline. Then I spread all the equipment on the tarp in front of the boat and photographed the imposing mound. I wanted that photographic record to prove, for anyone who cared, what an enormous amount of equipment my little kayak was going to have to carry.

By the time I had finished my photographic essay, it was noon, and the trains from Skagway and Whitehorse had pulled in. I had heard them approaching from a long way off, and I marveled again at the neat timing which allowed them to arrive in front of the Bennett station at almost exactly the same moment. Like lemmings, most of the passengers piled off and surged directly into the dining room. But a few took the time to come up to see the church before lunch, and, of course, they found me there, looking very busy in the midst of my equipment. I was wearing a grey felt hat, three days of beard, and was using a terribly melodramatic antler-handled hunting knife to cut the nylon line I was using to bind some of the equipment. (This was its most dangerous assignment during the trip.) The tourists seemed quite impressed, and I must admit that I couldn't help adopting what I hoped was the proper air for an experienced, intrepid outdoorsman. A few of them photographed me silently, as though I were a strange rock or flower they had to add to their photo collection, and one or two of them came up and spoke with me for a moment. They asked me where I was going, shook their heads, wished me well, and hurried back to their lunches.

After my visitors left, I could feel myself sliding from behind the facade of calm confidence I had put on for them. One man had explained to his wife that of course I was certainly a very experienced kayaker, as only such a person would dare to go on such a trip. I knew better about myself, and I found myself wondering if the man wasn't perhaps correct: That only an experienced kayaker *would* dare such a trip. My mood was not helped by the black clouds that were replacing the grey overcast. The boat was assembled, however, and the time had come. There was nothing more to do but carry it and my things from the church down to the water.

I made the transfer in four trips, the last in a sprinkling rain, and then put the boat into the water. The rain picked up, along with the wind, as I began to load the boat. I packed the tent first, sliding it way up into the bow, a difficult long push. I had tied a long cord to the tent so that it could be pulled out again fairly easily. Next came the canvas shoulder bag full of clothing in a plastic bag, which proved to be a tight fit in the narrow bow. After that, the foot pedals for the rudder lines had to be cinched onto the board on the bottom of the boat. Then I turned to the back of the boat, sliding a cardboard box of odds and ends far into the rear and following the box with the typewriter case of camera equipment, which went in directly behind the backrest of my seat.

The pack frame was next. I had re-packed the food into one of the long boat bags, and I cinched this bag to the frame along with the sleeping bag and the foam pad, which had been tied together and wrapped inside a plastic garbage bag. Finally I ended by stuffing everything else all about the cockpit of the boat. On the bottom, underneath my legs, went my charts, writing pad and the folded tarp. On each side and behind the cockpit, I bundled all the water bottles, the stove, a gas can or two, extra clothing and my boots. Then I shoved the ensolite pad on top of everything, hopefully to protect the miscellaneous equipment from all the mud and sand and water which invariably came into the cockpit with wet boots.

The boat was loaded to the bursting point—I actually wondered if I would also be able to fit inside it—and as I worked, I had to keep pushing it further and further from shore to keep it from grounding. As a result, I was standing in deeper and deeper water. And that water was *cold*!—actually about 36 degrees. Despite the rubber boots and woolen socks I was wearing, my feet were numb by the time I had finished the loading. As I jumped up and down on the shore to get them warm again, the thought began to seep into the corners of my mind that my plans for swimming to shore if the boat capsized were purely academic fantasies. I guessed that one's body would have perhaps four or five minutes to function in such water, and not many more minutes to live. I doubt very much that a person could swim 50 yards—certainly not more than 100—in such cold. Travel on the upper Yukon, then, especially on its broad lakes, presents the traveler with a "must-win" situation. You simply *must not* tip over.

Of course, if anyone ever really stopped to consider the risks involved in driving or riding in a car, I'm sure they would never drive or ride again. But we all employ a sort of double-think, a denial of reality and its dangers, and continue careening about the countryside. The same sort of mental shield came into play for me as I stood in that cold water. Without any further thought about what the cold water meant for my trip, I steadied the boat and prepared to get in. The lake was stippled with the light rainfall, and the trains at the station were still huffing and steaming, waiting for their passengers to reboard. The cockpit was cramped, very cramped, and the boat looked terribly overloaded and low in the water. But there was nothing I could do about it. It was time to go.

I was just settling down into the kayak, trying to fit myself into its cramped confines, when a sudden squall nearly blew me right out of the lake. The wind and rain seemed almost to have been waiting for just this moment to chastise me for my temerity; I can think of no other explanation for the incredible timing of the torrent. The lake's surface was swept by rolling white caps; I could see the foolishness of trying to start out in such weather. I pulled the boat halfway up onto the shore, closed the spray cover, and took refuge under a small tree near the edge of the lake to watch the squall rush by. Could the gods possibly be trying to tell me something, I wondered?

As I sat under the tree, the wind blowing the rain down the hill past me and out over the lake, I noticed that the trains were finally loading up to depart. But back by the baggage car of the train from Whitehorse, two figures were busy unloading mounds of equipment and an aluminum canoe. One of the men began carrying the equipment down to the beach by the water, and by

The Quisnam and my equipment.

the time the trains had left, the canoe was on its side on the beach, the equipment was piled beside it, and the two figures were back under the eaves of the station out of the rain. Fishermen on the lake? Fellow travelers? I was curious about the men and the canoe, but I wasn't in quite the mood for a talk in the rain just yet. So I left them to their own devices and ran for the nearest of the cabins for a drier haven.

After an hour or so, the rain and wind began to die down a little, and since I was cold and uncomfortable sitting on a broken table in the little cabin, I ran down to the station. The two newcomers were there, hunched under the eaves, staring out into the rain. One of them was large and hefty, the other shorter and lighter, both as roughly dressed and unshaven as I was. They smiled when I allowed that it seemed a little damp for boating, and we were quickly exchanging backgrounds. John, the short one, had planned his trip down the Yukon while on duty in Vietnam and had gotten his friend Randy to go along with him. They had driven up to Whitehorse, spent a week or two there waiting for word of the breakup of the ice on Bennett, and had just arrived to begin their trip down to the Bering Sea.

As we talked, I realized how much preparation these two had put into their trip. John continually referred to bits of information about the river and details of travel along it which I knew nothing about. We probed gently back and forth, trying to estimate each other's capabilities and experience, until the wind and rain slackened and finally stopped. The three of us then walked out from the station, John and Randy to look around the church and cabins while I walked back up the hill above the kayak for a look at the weather and the lake.

A few minutes later John and Randy wandered down to look at my kayak, heavily loaded and tiny-looking on the shore of the lake. I was pretty sure I could accurately guess their thoughts as they stood inspecting my overloaded craft, now and then shaking their heads as they talked. But I didn't need any sort of negative criticism or "helpful advice" at this point, so I waited at the top of the hill until they had walked back to their boat, which lay between mine and the station. Randy and John were pleasant enough, but they both radiated a certain hard-edged, aggressive competitiveness about the outdoors which rubbed me the wrong way, especially as it contrasted so heavily with my own lack of experience. John in particular seemed too eager to tell me how proficient he was. Randy was quieter, and I somehow felt more willing to grant him his due as a man at home in the woods.

I was startled at having such negative reactions to the first two people I should meet on my journey down the Yukon. Undoubtedly, a part of my reaction had to do with a sense of their intruding on *my* lake, and, by extension, on my adventure. In any case, although in retrospect it all seems a bit childish, I knew that I wanted to be on the lake before this pair, so that I would be ahead of them as a traveler on the Yukon headwaters, second only to the unknown traveler mentioned by the Indian workman. Thus as soon as Randy and John headed off toward their own boat, I hurried down the hill. The weather was clearing, no doubt about it, and there was nothing keeping me here.

I could hear the music of the ice shards again as I pulled the Quisnam off the shore and into the water, marveling once more at how heavy it felt. A minute later I made my second attempt to board the craft and begin the voyage. Perhaps the most dangerous moment in a kayak in terms of tipping over is that moment when you get in or out of it. The idea is to get one leg inside while the other supports you, smoothly lower your center of gravity by sitting down in the boat, then draw the other leg in. If you do all this quickly and efficiently it is very easy. But at this point

I was still awkward and hesitant, while the boat was cramped and full. I got in after a heart-stopping pitch or two back and forth, getting only about a cup of ice water down my boot in the process. The boat felt very heavy and unwieldy and was grounded back on the sand with my weight. I tucked the spray cover around myself, pushed the Quisnam back off the sand with the paddle, swung the craft around, and began to paddle very carefully along the shore of Bennett Lake.

John and Randy were busy getting their canoe loaded to go, so we simply waved and exchanged a few words. I forget exactly what was said, but I remember bristling a bit under the impression that their words implied that they felt I ought to wait for their company. I bristled because I was half thinking the same thing myself.

I paddled off energetically, trying for a certain flair of motion while keeping absolutely still so as not to tip the kayak over. I stayed prudently close to the right shore, but I was beginning to feel rather pleased with the progress I was making. The boat hadn't sunk yet, I hadn't collapsed from fatigue, and I seemed to be proceeding at a pretty good pace down the lake toward the band of "rotten ice." With a little luck I would be through the ice and on my way down the lake in no time.

In terms of scenery, the afternoon quickly became superb. The storm had moved down the lake between its mountain walls, so that ahead of me all was dark cloud and wet rock and water, while behind me the sun was lighting the snows of the Coast Range and giving warmth to my immediate surroundings. The water increased the depth of its icy blue-green color in the sunlight, and only little ripples roughed its surface.

When I reached the barrier of ice that stretched from my side of the lake clear across to the other shore, the sound of the icy wind chimes became louder. The whole rear fringe of the ice barrier proved to be made up of the tiny shards, gathered by the wind and current against the strand of ice, which was 100 feet or so wide. Beyond this first obstacle there was open water, then another broad stretch of ice. I paddled cautiously up to the ice, then back-paddled to stop my forward movement so that I might study the barrier. The shore was still nearby, which was psychologically reassuring, and the ice in front of me did indeed look "rotten." I stroked gently forward into the bobbing shards. The boat slid ahead easily, although the scraping and tearing sound of the ice bits against the hull was most unwelcome. But freezing water did not come rushing in on me, so I decided that the hull must be equal to the punishment. I continued the hard work of paddling forward, pushing pounds of floating ice behind me to gain my forward motion.

As I proceeded, I saw that shards of a slightly different consistency lay on each side of me. They had what looked like a film of ice holding them together. I pushed the paddle into one of these sheets of ice fragments and discovered with a shock which nearly broke the paddle that these fragments were frozen into a solid pan of ice a foot thick. It was a bit unnerving to discover that I was moving down a very narrow channel of loose ice shards floating between heavy pans of ice—in a boat of wood, canvas and thin rubber weighing a grand 50 pounds. This in itself wouldn't have been all that bad, but I also noticed that the pans on each side of me were moving together, causing the shards floating in between to bunch up in front of me. At several tons each, the pans held a considerable advantage over my delicate little boat. It was time to get out of there!

I backed water and shards desperately, gained a few feet back toward the open water I had come from, then headed off through another narrow channel toward shore. I am not quite clear on what happened during the next several minutes, but somehow I got the boat near the shore and scrambled out to stamp a channel through the ice, so that I could pull the boat along to the open water several yards ahead. I don't know which was more chilling, the horrible crunching sounds which came from the boat as it rode over the broken ice, or the knee-deep icy water I was sloshing through, but I tried to ignore both. I had to get the kayak to open water, safely away from the ice pans which were beginning to grind and crush together before the increasingly stiff wind sweeping down the lake.

With a final pull, the kayak crunched over the last of the shards by the shore and floated again in the stretch of clear water between the first band of ice I had just passed through and the much longer stretch of ice covering the lake 200 yards ahead. I grounded the kayak on a little sandy beach cupped in a tiny point of land jutting off from the railroad tracks, emptied my boots of the ice water, then looked up to see John and Randy just approaching the ice and going through the same set of emotions I had experienced in entering the ice floe. They rode right on into the shards, discovered the solid ice waiting for them, then realized that they could be in a difficult situation. However, surrounded by aluminum, they apparently felt considerably more confident of the strength of their craft, and they began bulling on through. They seemed to be making good headway until they struck a solid causeway·

View over the ice barrier on Bennett Lake, toward Mt. Hoffmann on right, Mt. Cleveland on left, and the Chilkoot Pass between.

of ice blocking their exit to the open water. Incredibly, Randy produced a full-sized ax from the canoe—these guys were equipped!—and proceeded to hack the channel open.

I was back in the kayak by now, and I paddled down to the next ice field. John and Randy had cleared the first strand of ice and were a few dozen yards behind me. After one look at how thick this ice was, however, and how much there was of it, I finally realized that my canvas and rubber boat simply would not do as an icebreaker. I turned around and paddled back toward the narrow strip of sandy beach by the tracks. Because of the Indian workman's warning about the dangers of the middle of the lake, I was surprised to hear John and Randy talking about going across the lake, to get to what looked like a better campsite on the other side. The lake was roughly a half mile wide here, and the water was fairly smooth, so I was briefly tempted to turn around and cross the lake myself. But some note of caution or fatigue sounded in my brain, and I continued to the shore.

It was well that I did and that Randy and John had not yet embarked on the long crossing; for when Randy chopped through the first causeway of ice, he must have taken out the lynchpin which held the whole strand of ice in place before the wind. The entire lake-wide mass of ice suddenly came free and began to slide down the lake toward John and Randy. They saw it coming in time and came hurrying back to my beach just as the channel, open and calm a moment before, closed behind them with startling speed. A few minutes later, all three of us were standing together on the little beach, watching in amazement as the combined ice floes ground down the lake before the wind.

As we stood there in silence, I found myself wondering about this first day of travel on Bennett. Were the gods trying to tell me something along the lines of "Go back, you fool!"? What if I had set out a few minutes earlier, before that first rain squall, and had been in the water with my overloaded, unbalanced kayak when the storm finally broke? What if I had not managed to get the kayak out from between the ice pans when they came grinding together, or if I or my companions had been out in the middle of the lake, a quarter mile from either shore, when the first ice strand broke loose and surged across the open channel? None of these things had happened, but there was no real reason why they might not have. I had been lucky three times that day, my first on the Yukon. Such thoughts gave me considerable pause.

Before I arrived on the shore of Bennett Lake, I had wrestled with the images of all sorts of dangers. Now, in just an hour or two on the upper Yukon, I had encountered some very real, possibly deadly hazards. Earlier in dealing with my fantasies, and now in the face of dangerous reality, I arrived at the same conclusion: We all owe life a death, and I think I can accept mine more easily if it should come while I am doing something enjoyable, if dangerous, rather than while I am trudging through one or another of life's mundane routines. It seemed to me a valuable realization that I could not and would not treasure my life to the point of complete timidity—seeking safety and surety and avoiding all challenge and chance. I doubt that such thoughts ever arise for a truly adventurous person, but for me they were an important development in the on-going education which this trip provided.

Of course, all of this sounds terribly melodramatic in the face of what is undeniably one of the world's tamer adventures—especially as I am here, after the fact, intact and writing all of this down. It also suggests that I traveled the length of the Yukon holding a skull and muttering "Alas, poor Yorick," which could hardly have been further from the truth. John, Randy and I stood on the sand laughing over the predicament we had nearly gotten ourselves into, then set off for a walk down the railroad tracks to take a closer look at the ice, which the wind and current had managed to move a good 800 paces down the lake.

To the right of the tracks, away from the lake, the thick brush and small second-growth pines (all the hillsides about this upper end of Bennett Lake were completely stripped of their trees by the would-be gold miners for lumber for their jury-rigged boats) grew thickly, sweeping up the sloping flanks of the surrounding peaks toward the tree-line far above. Just a few yards down from our sandy point of shoreline, a burbling waterfall tumbled down a rocky channel set into the hillside and flowed under the tracks into the icy lake. The sun was warm and covered everything with its setting gold. It was a very pleasant afternoon.

We reached the rear edge of the ice at a point where the tracks angled around an outcropping of rock and curved away around a slight two-mile-long bay on the narrow upper end of Bennett Lake. The ice filled this bay from side to side, apparently held here by a jam of some sort at the far end, where the walls of the lake narrowed in again. The ice pans, pushed by the wind coming down the lake, were sliding and circling along almost in slow motion, shifting and re-shifting to fill the surface of the bay more and more tightly.

John and Randy soon grew tired of the scene and left to set up camp, but I stayed and sat on a boulder just above the water, to watch the ice like a spectator at some great migration. On the lake surface before me, the pans wheeled and turned before the wind, and the sun, reflected by the pans and shards in between, sent glints of white and gold and very light green flashing in every direction. Many of the pans were huge, but they all seemed to move gently, even politely, as they shifted and packed the bay. As I watched, a great flat pan, nearly round and 30 yards across, came pirouetting along the shore, catching one corner and then another on the rocks to spin slowly on with graceful elegance, its dance performed to the music of the clinking ice shards all about.

It suddenly turned cold as the sun finally slipped behind the high walls of the Bennett Range directly across the lake, and I hiked back up the tracks to our cove. I found John industriously shaving a stick of wood for kindling, looking as though he next intended to pull out a bow and arrow to start the fire the proper way. I was surprised when he accepted a splash of white gas from me, since many purists frown on such a means to start a fire. I brought out some crackers and blue cheese, which John appreciated enormously, and he and Randy reciprocated with a few of their snack items.

While the night grew deeper, the three of us talked a good deal, in a perfectly friendly fashion, but in the course of that evening and the following day I found myself becoming more and more uneasy with my companions. Some of the problem lay with the fact that I most certainly had not been expecting company this early in the trip, and my systems for travel and camping were not really ready to be put on display. But I also felt a sense of one-upmanship being practiced each time John produced one of his suggestions for my benefit:

"You mean you don't have a candle to help light that stove? You really should have one like this."

"You tie your tent down that way? Here, let me show you a better knot for that."

"Don't you have anything more to eat than crackers and nuts? (I did.) Let us give you some hot dogs."

I could feel my ire rising at each of these suggestions even as I recognized their validity. John, for example, did show me a very useful knot, and I tied it on everything all down the river. But somehow the way it was given galled me.

Another thing that bothered me was the aggressive way in which these two approached their surroundings. John had pulled out a mean-looking .22 with a telescopic sight for our walk down the tracks, on the off chance that he might be able to "bag something for dinner," and they both appeared eager to crunch off into the woods and blast whatever happened to be moving about there. Three days further down the lake, in Carcross, John invited me to join them in an epic feed on a stew-pot full of squirrels they had just shot. Since I feel any squirrel has more right to its life than I to its meat, this rather set me back. I am certainly not consistent in this outlook, as the vegetarians have yet to win me away from enjoying a steak or good chop, but I do think that a wild animal alive is worth much more than one dead in a freezer or cooking pot, unless its meat is absolutely necessary to survival. Since John and Randy were carrying food for about a year, I found their behavior less than admirable.

John and Randy seemed to be equipped for contingencies I had never even thought of, and being so well equipped they tended to imply that anyone less equipped probably couldn't make the trip. Since at this point I had no solid proof to the contrary, all the display of pistols (sealed by law in Canada), rifles, axes, hunting knives and survival belts did not help my peace of mind. How could I possibly manage a journey that required such massive armament, when all my weaponry consisted of three flares, a hunting knife, and perhaps my camera lenses, which I might throw at the goblins as they came for me?

What upset me by far the most of anything on the entire trip down the river, including Five Finger Rapids, was a conversation that I somehow got into with John that first night:

"You know," John said, "one thing that amazes me about you guys who travel alone is the possible medical problems that might come up." He had just finished describing the medical kit they were carrying, which included penicillin, novacaine, and probably the operating theater of the Mayo Clinic. My medical kit, as you will recall, consisted of a small bag of aspirins, band-aids and suntan lotion. "I mean," he exclaimed dramatically, "do you know how to tie off an artery?"

"No, I can't say as I do," I muttered, not at all liking how this conversation was progressing. I mean, for God's sake, tie off an artery!?

"Oh, well," he went on, "you could always just apply a tourniquet. You'd probably lose the limb, but there are a lot of things a person can do these days without an arm or a leg."

And he was serious! Even now I am speechless in the face of these lines. How do you even begin to deal with such sentiments? I was disappointed that my reaction to my first acquaintances on the river should be so strong and so negative; one very good reason for my making this trip was to get away from exactly these kinds of "city" emotions. But perhaps it was just as well that all these errant feelings did arise then at the start of the trip. I could refer to my memory of the frictions of these first two days as an emotional bench mark against which I might measure the degree of calm and repose that I hoped my travels in the wilderness would produce.

As the evening wore on, we talked by the warm fire built at the base of several rocks for protection against the cold night wind. John spoke at length of his plans for moving to Alaska and opening up an ecology preserve in connection with getting an M.A. or Ph.D. in biology from the University of Alaska. He also told of his idea of giving lectures on the Yukon to school children around his home near Chicago. I am sure John could pull all this off if he decided to. While his personality and some of his attitudes seemed almost perfectly designed to raise my emotional hackles, I found myself greatly admiring John's self-confidence and glibness, as well as the nature of his plans for the future.

The temperature began to drop until it was simply too far below the range of comfort to be ignored. We killed the fire and crawled into our tents, which were only six feet from the tracks because there was no other flat place for them. Not much later all three of us were back outside again, chasing a porcupine that Randy had heard nosing about, the first wildlife of any size that I had seen on the trip. We ran about in our bare feet and finally cornered the frightened animal in a rocky crevice on the slope above the tracks. John slapped the animal with a glove, to get some of its quills for heaven knows what, and then we left the animal in peace.

As I lay dozing in my tent—that little cavern of security that tends to turn everything beyond its confines into a dangerous "out there,"—I couldn't decide whether things were going well for me or not. There I was, trapped by ice, unable to tie off an artery, and now faced with marauding porcupines. I finally concluded that my "plight" was not going to be solved through further thought and fell promptly and soundly asleep. A few hours later I was nearly blown out of the tent by a monster ore train that hurtled past six feet away from my head. The engineer apparently feared that we might not notice his passage, so he made sure of our attention by leaning on his horn. Another lesson learned: If you can avoid it, don't sleep too near the railroad tracks!

The next morning, June 8, the ice was still there, blocking all forward progress. The wind had blown its trailing edge about 1,000 yards down the lake, and the ice sheet seemed to be nearly continuous now, with none of the open spaces of water which had patched the icefield the afternoon before. I learned this by walking down the tracks soon after waking up.

When I got back to the camp, John and Randy were making preparations to cross the lake to the more inviting forested campsites on the far side. They asked if I wanted to come over, but I declined, despite the prospect of at least another day and night on this narrow slip of land and the passage of another roaring ore train. The sudden halt forced by the ice had halted all my energy and initiative as well; I just didn't want to bother changing my camp if I couldn't move forward. In fact, I found I could hardly be bothered to move myself about the camp I had. For most of the morning after John and Randy pushed off, I slouched down out of the wind behind a warm rock and read a book on the history of Zen in Japan.

Toward noon, I heard faint voices floating across the lake and realized that John and Randy were yelling to me. Their voices were tiny but their words were clearly amplified across the half mile of water by the sheer rocky walls that curved behind them. They shouted that they had found an excellent campsite and wanted me to join them. I thought about their suggestion for a while, decided that I had nothing better to do, and finally worked up the energy to hop into my nearly empty kayak and paddle across.

The kayak felt totally different without the great weight of my equipment. It fairly skipped its way across the mirror-smooth lake, which was much wider than I expected; I could see why people warned against getting caught in its middle. The camp my companions had found was indeed excellent, but when John began to head off into the woods with the .22 in his hand and a survival belt and knife strapped to his waist, I lost even the slight desire I felt to join them. Before he disappeared into the trees, John squatted down at the edge of the trees, studied something intently that lay on the ground, then sagely muttered "Wolverine droppings" and went on his way. I stayed only a short while longer, since I had the excuse that the wind was beginning to kick up little waves on the lake's surface.

When I got back to my campsite, I settled in my spot against the warm rock and tried to resume my reading. I couldn't concentrate, however, and kept gazing off at my spectacular surroundings. To my left, back up the lake behind Bennett Station, the sun was warm and bright on the Boundary Range and the Chilkoot Pass, which stood out with great clarity against the backdrop of storm clouds over the Pacific. Before me the lake was stirring in the afternoon wind and darkened by the shadows which crept toward me from Randy and John's side of the lake, where the afternoon sun was cut off by the sheer ramparts of the Bennett Range. And to the right I could still see the formidable line of white, a little under a mile away, which was holding me in this small pocket by the railroad tracks.

My emotions were in a strange state. I was still wrestling with the negative vibrations of my encounter with John and, less markedly, with Randy. I was also feeling that sense of loss and worry one inevitably feels when someone who has unexpectedly joined you in an unfamiliar setting leaves you again. Before they arrive you don't need anyone, are complete in yourself; but after they have come and gone, you feel a little empty and defenseless against the world around you. I couldn't pinpoint what was worrying me; it felt like a return of the formless fears I had experienced before actually reaching Bennett Lake.

I finally decided that the main cause for my discontent was the frustration and aggravation of inaction. My trip down the Yukon had been blocked before I had really even begun, and for all I knew, the ice might stay on the lake for weeks. It certainly looked capable of it. And there I was, trapped within sight of my starting point, and only six feet from the railroad tracks that had carried me into this wilderness.

I began to get mad. I hadn't come all this way just to have a little ice stop me. If it insisted on staying on that bay on the lake, well then I would just carry all my things around it. I came up here to travel and, damn it, that was what I was going to do. I felt much better as this resolve took shape in my mind, and I immediately set about putting it into action.

The first thing I did was to walk back down the tracks again to check on the distances involved in outflanking the ice. As I walked, I counted off the paces and found that the back edge of the ice was now 1,200 yards down the lake, jammed even more firmly into the small bay. I then walked around the curve of the bay, stepping off the 2,300 paces around the ice to open water beyond—quite a distance to lug 150 pounds of boat and equipment. However, 1,600 yards down the tracks, there was still a long narrow channel of open water along the shoreline which led almost to the head of the ice. If the shoreline was still open the next day, I could carry the heavier equipment clear beyond the ice and then would only have to cart the dismantled kayak the 1,600 yards to the start of that channel, where I could reassemble it and then paddle down to the head of the ice. There I would simply carry the equipment and the intact kayak to the open water a hundred feet or so further ahead, load up again, and be on my way.

As I stood at the head of the ice making my plans, I could see how it had come to jam in on the lake at this point; on both my side and the far shore the ice had buckled and piled itself up on the beaches as the shores of the broad bay pinched in again and forced the wind-blown ice into a narrower portion of the lake. The wind blew down on the ice floe from the rear and the waves rocked the pans, but so far this ice at the head of the floating white mass had held fast, blocking both the ice and my progress. But tomorrow would see the end of that, I thought joyfully, and once beyond this ice I was going to fly!

I slept almost soundly that night, nearly managing to work the night freight into my dreams. The next morning I woke about seven, eager to set about my plan of action. I didn't know it then, but my diary entry for this day was going to start with the words "Well, its been kind of an interesting day, so far. The sort that builds character, I guess." It was chilly when I got up, but the sky was clear and the sun soon warmed the day to a respectable spring temperature. After a breakfast of Grapenuts and milk, I packed my tent and sleeping equipment into the boat and paddled down to the ice.

During the night the wind had blown the ice a little further into the bay, so that I was able to swing around a rocky point and into a small cove directly behind the ice. I took everything out of and off the boat and dumped the equipment near the railroad tracks, then carried the boat up as well. In order to carry my things I had to take my pack frame off the back of the boat, and it pained me to untie all the intricate fastenings which held it. But there was nothing else to be done.

I first carried all my heaviest things, including my camera case and the shoulder bag of clothing, down the tracks to the very head of the ice 2,300 yards away. The second load of odds and ends went 1,600 yards down the tracks, to the start of the channel along the shore, which was still open despite the night's wind. And then came my great triumph: Unable to bear the thought of taking the Quisnam completely apart, I strapped the pack frame onto the coaming structure of the cockpit, lifted the whole load across my back, and staggered off down the tracks with the 15-foot kayak stretching from the rock walls on my right well out over the shore on my left. I would have been in considerable trouble with my awkward load if either a train or one of the zippy little maintenance cars that rocketed past once or twice a day had snuck up on me from around one of the curves of the bay.

But at this point, I was too happy to care. I had made a considerable effort, which in itself seemed something of an achievement. Moreover, it was going to gain me open water, despite the ice. And once on that water I was really going to ramble. In a great burst of feeling and triumph I found myself joyfully shaking my fist at the ice and the mountains and the sky, bellowing out as loud as I could "I'm going to make it, by Christ. I'm going to make it."

This was the first outright mistake of the trip. Hubris, as you will recall from your reading of Greek plays and philosophy, is the term given to the overweening pride that mortals showed before the gods put them in their place. Men, the Greeks felt, were not meant to show pride on such a scale that it might offend the gods above. And I find that I rather believe in this principle. It does seem as though "pride goeth before the fall." But for a moment I had forgotten this reality. My lesson was not long in coming.

As I was carrying the kayak along the tracks beside the ice, the wind began to come up, jostling the ice. By the time I reached the start of the open channel along the ice floe, got the boat down the bank and into the water, put the pack frame back on, and loaded it with all the things from my second carry, the whole plain of ice was clearly moving. I paddled down the channel as quickly as I could, but by the time I got near the head of the ice, the whole sheet of ice had moved forward before the wind, jamming further into the narrows beyond the bay. My short portage was a long one now. To emphasize their displeasure with me, the gods also banished the sun behind scudding rain clouds, and the afternoon became flat and grey and cold.

I was still determined to try to outrun the ice, so I dragged the boat up onto the shore away from any rampant ice pans and then ran with all the loose stuff in the kayak down to my first pile of things. Dropping what I was carrying, I raced back to the kayak, yanked it up into the air, and ran with it down the tracks toward the head of the jam. The kayak, held over my head, swayed and threatened to pitch off into the rocks—ever tried running in a strong wind with a 15-foot, 50 pound kayak over your head?—but I managed to make it to a spot where the water was still clear. Then it was run fast, really fast, back to the equipment, grab up as much of it as possible, and make it back to the boat while there was still time and open water in which to launch it.

Only I didn't have the time, and I finally knew it. As I stood on the shore by the kayak, the wind whipping past and rain beginning to fall, the ice floe came free again and began to surge through the narrows beyond the bay. To add to the occasion, a puckish burst of wind blew off the floppy hat I was wearing, swept it along the beach and out over the water, and deposited it neatly on an ice cake. Such insult piled on injury was simply too much. I was not going to let that hat get away! I took off my boots and socks, put on my rubber boots, grabbed a paddle and waded knee-deep into the freezing water. The boots were 15 inches high, so this put them a good 6 inches under water and, of course, filled them to the brim. With a long stretch of the oar I snagged the pan of ice and again possessed my miserable hat.

It took only a few minutes to get my socks and boots back onto my frozen feet, but in that short time I had the distinct displeasure of seeing the trailing ice of the floe, which I had left a mile behind earlier in the day, blow completely by me, leaving a vista of open water in its wake. The gods must have been in a playful mood. With a flick of their windy fingers, they had removed the barrier which had caused my day's effort, completely invalidating the plans I had made, the miles I had walked and the heavy loads I had carried. But perhaps their little joke had been a blessing in disguise. I am not sure how pleasant or safe it would have been paddling out in front of the ice when the wind blew it out of its jam and sent it rifling down the surface of the lake.

The rain was beginning to get serious, so I gathered my things together up by the railroad tracks, covered them with the tarp, turned the kayak over, and then crawled under the tarp and watched a kind of natural morality play going on down by the shoreline of the lake. Chunks of ice had been left stranded in shallow water when the wind cleared this section of the lake of its icy cover, and now the wind and waves of the lake seemed to work as a vengeful team against these poor weak remnants of the winter, pinning them against the shoreline rocks, blowing water over them, tearing at them ceaselessly, until they were reduced from solid chunks to spidery shards to nothing in a surprisingly short time. And with the lake waters before me clear of ice, for the first time in eight months, the waves seemed to revel in their new freedom.

When the rain slacked off, I wandered down the tracks a half mile or so, passing a partially ruined building filled with a huge rusting boiler and several bags of trash. My destination was a rocky hill between the tracks and the water, where I was pleased to be unable to see the ice which had so recently been blocking my progress. The wind whipping about me was certainly strong enough to blow the ice right out of the water, and I hoped that it had.

The blustering wind was cold even through all my layers of clothing, and the chilling rain was still misting down, so I climbed a hill beyond the tracks to huddle under the protection of a grove of trees and record the day's events in the legal pad I was using as a diary. It was several minutes before I noticed that there was a rusty iron stake in the ground next to my foot, with a chain leading from it to the gaping jaws of a trap, half hidden in the pine needles. What else could I possibly need to make my day complete?

At last the rain ceased completely, and I went back to the boat. Even then it was not very late in the evening, and it was still bright enough for me to see Bennett Station, my departure point of two days before. I couldn't stand it; I simply had to get in some further travel. I loaded up the boat and, with some difficulty, managed to get myself into it and out into the substantial waves that were sweeping north down the lake. The problem was that I was at the narrowest point of the lake, the point where the ice had jammed, and the wind and waves were particularly forceful here. They also traveled at a slight angle to the steep and rocky shore, so that I had to work across the waves at an angle in order to keep clear of the rocks. I felt that if I could just get around the corner of the narrows, several hundred yards away, I would be somewhat protected from the wind and able to travel in relative ease. But the waves, or rollers really, tended to turn the kayak broadside as they passed, and with the kayak as heavily loaded as it was, each wave that broke over it made the boat tip and sway and pitch.

I found myself struggling fairly desperately to prevent a broach. After 200 frantic yards, I had had more than enough. I got the boat to shore, splashed out, and unceremoniously jerked it out of the breaking waves. I was beginning to wonder if I would never get out of sight of my starting point at Bennett Station. I lugged

The kayak on Bennett Lake, after walking it around the ice.

my food and sleeping things across the tracks to the delapidated building I had seen earlier on my walk. A bit of remaining roof in one corner provided some shelter against the rain that began to drizzle down again, and for that I was quite willing to share my quarters with the several loads of garbage strewn about. I was cold and my feet were wet, but a cup of tea, a little food, and a bed platform rigged up from old boards without too many rusty nails helped set things right.

I woke often during the night, almost every hour, to make sure the boat was still perched safely on the rocks above the water. I also found that I had to rouse myself every now and then to drive the rodents away from my food supplies, and to inform one especially impertinent fellow that he was making a mistake when he came up on my sleeping bag to find out whether *I* was edible. And when I wasn't occupied in these pursuits, I found myself wide awake anticipating the arrival of the early morning freight. Another peaceful night in the wilderness!

5   Advance and Victory

After fidgeting and cat-napping through the darkest hours of the night, I finally got up for the last time at three a.m. The wind had dropped and the water in the narrows outside the broken door of my shelter was still and calm and serenely beautiful. It was uncanny how different the lake proved to be during this day in comparison to the first three days I had spent on it. In fact, this fourth day of my trip, June 10, must stand with two or three others as the most beautiful of the entire journey.

I carried my bedding and food bag back down to the boat and strapped them onto the frame on the back, then marvelled once again at how strong the Quisnam was proving to be, as I yanked and hauled it off the rocks and back into the water. It certainly was not receiving gentle treatment. For the first time in three days there was no sign of ice barring my way as far as I could see down the lake. It was a pleasure to slip into the cockpit of the kayak that morning, knowing that I would be able to put in a reasonable day's travel at last. The kayak itself even felt more responsive and alert than it had before, perhaps because my loading of it had become somewhat better with practice.

As I began to paddle down the shoreline of the lake, the rising sun was just brushing a glow onto the snow of the mountain summits to the east, while I moved in deep shadow, far below the heights. The lake was slightly choppy in the narrows, but it became glassy smooth, like still ink, as the shoreline of the lake began to curve into broad bays and tree-covered points on my right. The kayak sliced an unending wake which V-ed away behind me through the expanding circles of my paddle strokes. It was perfectly quiet, so quiet that I could often hear the sounds of the paddles echoing back to me from the rocky walls of the shoreline.

I had been paddling for an hour or two when the early morning freight train with its dozens of ore cars came hurtling up the lake from Whitehorse and Carcross. As it sped past me I was surprised, and very pleased, when the engineer gave a great wave of his hand and tooted out a happy salutation on the engine's whistle. He seemed to be applauding my efforts and my final success at getting past the ice at the head of Bennett, as though he had been watching over me and was aware of my frustration. He also may have been sharing with me the beauty and pleasure of the crisp clear morning. I lifted the paddle over my head in both hands and shook it in a sign of victory and agreement. The engineer hooted his reply and then the train was gone around the upper end of the bay, although I could hear its progress for many minutes longer.

Five miles down the lake from my early morning start, I passed a two-story building of brick beside the railroad tracks which carried the elegant name of Paddington on the maps. The sun was just able to touch me here through a gap in the hills of the lake, and I hoped that the man I saw moving about might see me paddling by and invite me in for breakfast. In fact, he did come out onto the wooden deck leading down to the water, but when I had swung the boat around and paddled back to where he stood, he didn't notice the hungry look I assumed and confined his conversation to the weather and my questions about the ice.

Speaking with a very Canadian accent—not too surprising, I suppose, in Canada—he said that the storm of the night before had blown the ice all the way down the lake. However, he thought that there might still be some ice blocking the lake's outlet at Carcross. I thanked him and moved on, to enjoy a solitary breakfast on a gravel spit that pushed out to connect a rocky island with the shore. After eating my breakfast of cereal and instant milk mixed in a tin cup, I walked out to the island and climbed up to its top. I found a faded wooden cross there, stark against the blue skyline and the surrounding rocks. I have no idea what the grave held, but I couldn't help but wonder if the cross marked the lonely grave of some gold-seeker of 74 years ago—or perhaps the body of the last kayaker to pass this way. Returning to the boat, I stood and stretched for a moment, then noticed that from a distance the boat appeared to be lying on rocks. The water beneath was so clear it seemed almost invisible.

I embarked again and paddled on, still in the deep shadows of the early morning hours. It was chilly, but I didn't realize how cold it really was until I reached forward to brush the water drops from the surface of the canvas deck. I discovered that they were frozen solid. It was too beautiful a day for it to be so cold, I thought, and in agreement with my thoughts, the sun finally rose above the peaks surrounding the lake and I was able to begin peeling off some layers of clothing. As the sun grew warmer and my clothing less cumbersome, I also slipped into a steady paddling rhythm, one of the best I held during all the trip. With it, I

Spectator.

was able to cover what I realize in retrospect were prodigious distances for me, with very little sense of exertion. I would pick out a point ahead, paddle as many strokes as were needed to reach it, then pick out the next point and head for it in turn. The miles rolled by, one after another, until by the end of the day I had covered 22 miles of still lake water.

The passage of miles was marked by a metamorphosis of the landscape. It changed from the extremely impressive, rugged mountain peaks which tower over Bennett Station, to lower peaks and then high hills which drew back from the lake's edge, opening up vistas into the country behind the lake. Finally, by the time I had reached Carcross, I felt like I was in a completely different region from that at the head of the lake, one running more to plains and low hills rather than high alpine settings. All this change occurs in a mere 25 miles of lake, as it follows a slight S pattern between Bennett and Carcross. It is very impressive to cover those miles in a small boat, so that you can absorb the changing pattern of your surroundings slowly.

Another metamorphosis was going on at the same time that the landscape was changing, this one having to do with my hands. A kayak paddle comes in two sections, one socketing inside the other so that the edges of the blades are at right angles to each other. The reason the blades are set this way is so that the blade out of the water will slide easily through the air without resistance. The angles of the blades require a constant rotation of the grip for each stroke, and as I was to discover, this motion of skin against wood can produce blisters in record time. Another small lesson: Don't leave your gloves in the clothing bag. Luckily, I wasn't enough aware of the incipient blisters to distract from my remarkable surroundings.

I stopped for a lunch of crackers, blue cheese, and gobs of honey, margarine and jelly near a bubbling stream that ran under the railroad tracks and over a spit of gravel to the lake. A fat bossy ground squirrel informed me that that particular area belonged exclusively to him, but he proved amenable to a visitor after a friendly bribe of a cracker. While we were both munching noisily, the noon train from Whitehorse came rolling by, the windows filled with curious faces peering out at the strange apparition in rubber boots and beard. I waved at them all, and many waved back. It seemed to me that I was waving across a great gap to an entirely different and remote world, and undoubtedly it seemed the same for them.

A few minutes after I had returned to the lake, I was startled by the unmistakable cry of someone calling for help some distance away to my left. I turned the kayak in that direction, adrenalin coursing through my body, when the cry came again from my right. I turned the boat again and finally spotted one source of the cries of dispair. And with this hint I managed to locate the other on my left: Two loons were swimming on the lake on each side of me, calling back and forth with the strangest set of bird sounds I have ever heard. The nearer of the two noticed the weaving pattern of the kayak, and my evident confusion, and produced a lunatic laugh at their successful trick. I realize that this is a classic example of anthropomorphizing animal behavior, yet I can't put any other description on it: That bird laughed its head off at me and my discomfiture. Another loon, on Lake LaBerge, did the same thing when I tried to follow its darting underwater course. These loons were the first I had ever encountered, and I found them enormously interesting, with their amazing variety of cries and their beady, red-rimmed and staring mad eyes.

I left the loons to their cackling and proceeded down the smooth lake waters, now so still and of such a perfect reflective surface that I could see the surrounding hillsides and mountains just as well in the water as when I looked up at them. Behind me, my

A luncheon companion.

course disrupted this perfect stillness, and if I stopped, my own wake passed ahead of me and shattered the mountains and fluffy white clouds into bits and pieces. By mid-afternoon, when the snow-capped and rugged peaks that stood about Bennett's head had given way to lower, rolling green hills sweeping back from the lake's edge, I turned a slight corner to the right and saw Carcross waiting ahead of me. The town lay spread out in a line at the termination of Lake Bennett, where the shores pinch together and leave only a narrow channel, crossed by a railroad bridge and another for autos. The buildings of the town seemed very small and insignificant, set as they were before a backdrop of huge undulating hills and valleys that gave great depth to the scene.

As I paddled forward, I realized that I was seeing a familiar white line on the water between the town and myself. But there was something different about this ice: It had a boat stuck in the middle of it. I did a double take, but there was no denying that a canoe, sporting a very bright blue sail, was sitting 50 or 60 feet in from the back edge of the huge sheet of jammed ice pans. I paddled to the edge of the ice and shouted "Hello. Are you all right?" to the figure lying on one elbow at the back of the canoe.

The man in the canoe jerked around, startled, then a broad grin creased his blond beard and he waved and shouted back "Yes. Hello. I'm Rich Haupt. I've been expecting you." I didn't understand this remark until Rich explained that the railroad crews had been keeping him posted on my progress down the lake. He even knew that I was carrying a typewriter case, although the railroad workers had not been able to tell him that it carried camera equipment rather than a typewriter.

"I'm Gene Cantin," I called back. "I heard about you at the other end of the lake. But I certainly didn't expect to find you in the middle of more of this ice."

"Well, I decided I'd make it through today or else," he explained, then added ruefully, "But the wind hasn't come up. I thought it would drive me right through, and now I don't seem to be going anywhere."

Rich was wearing wrap-around dark glasses, a brown shirt, jeans and tennis shoes and looked as though he belonged more on a Hollywood street corner than in the middle of an ice jam on Bennett Lake. He had waited over 20 days at Bennett to begin his trip down the Yukon, the icy conditions belying the hopeful words "Yukon Summer" painted on the side of his canoe. Finally, he had set out down the lake, roping his boat down the shallows at the edge of the lake as the ice first began to melt, until he was halted by the thicker ice jammed at Carcross.

My presence seemed to bring Rich out of his lethargy, and as I left him to go to shore, he began to attack his foe again. For the next five or six hours, Rich forced his canoe along through the ice, rocking it, shoving with his feet, rowing at the ice with a rudder board, and yanking the sail back and forth for the few inches of gain it gave him toward the open water. There was at least a half mile of ice jammed in front of Carcross that day, and Rich eventually fought his way right through the middle of it.

I unloaded the boat, piled everything on a tarp some distance back from the ice, then lifted the boat itself out of the water and away from any possible danger from moving ice pans. Then, hungry for the surroundings of a town and hoping to mail out some letters explaining my delay on the lakes, I walked down the tracks into Carcross. As I went I paced off the distance and found that I had a 1,200-yard portage of all my equipment if I meant to get it past not only the ice jam Rich was stuck in but also the ice blocks collected in the struts of the railroad bridge crossing the outlet. I doubted that I would have the strength to make the

Haupt hard at work, conquering the ice jam at Carcross.

move that evening; I was beginning to feel the effects of the distance I had covered down the lake and the lack of sleep the night before.

Carcross was a strange but appealing little town. It sprawled out on both sides of the channel that drains Bennett into much smaller Nares Lake, and it consisted mainly of numerous small wooden cabins housing the largely Indian population. The town center sported an old wooden train station, Matthew Watson's General Store, the Caribou Hotel and a huge paddle-wheeler named the "Tutshi," pulled high up on the left bank of the channel. The bridge of the Tutshi proved to be the highest point in Carcross, higher than any of the several church steeples that poked up into the air from here and there among the cabins.

The Tutshi is one of the few survivors of a great fleet of steamers —250 at one point—that once plied the Yukon during its busy years. As recently as 1958, the white boat still cruised the upper lakes of the Yukon. Then a change in the ferry schedule on the Inland Passage to Skagway made it impractical for anyone to land there, take the train to Carcross, and enjoy a romantic meander on the Tutshi. A hunting-party outfitter told me that the boat was in mint condition when it was pulled out of the water in 1958. But like the Pyramids and the Colosseum, the Tutshi has proved an irresistable temptation to any nearby resident in need of building materials, and now its parts can be found all over Carcross. Today it is in sorry condition, a major task for the Yukon Historical Society that hopes to restore it.

After inspecting the Tutshi I headed for Matthew Watson's General Store, a few hundred feet away. I didn't really need to buy anything at that moment, but nonetheless I found myself almost compulsively striding in the front door, starting a routine that held true all down the river. If there was a store of any sort, I would not only go into it as though it were a matter of duty, I would also buy something even if I had no need for it whatsoever. Somehow, merely being in a store, with all its shelves of things to eat, brought a sense of relief and joy to me after being away from one for days on end. So much for escaping civilization and immersing oneself in nature: Undoubtedly all of this had something to do with the constant tutelage in the art of buying unnecessary things that we all go through every day in our modern urban society.

No matter what the reason, this first store that I encountered on the river—and its proprietor—proved fascinating. Matthew Watson's store was a strange hodge-podge of old and new, useful and useless items for sale. Matthew himself was a strange, frenetic man of 60 or 70 years of age; it almost seemed as though someone had wound up bony Mr. Watson to play at 78 rpm's while the rest of us move about at 45. He stomped about the store, rushing here and there, barking out a comment or an unrequested price for some item I was inspecting. The most treasured item in the high-ceilinged, cluttered and dusty store must have been the portion of a round of cheese carefully displayed in a weathered glass case. It looked as though it had come over the Chilkoot Pass with the original rushers of '98. I stood looking down at it for a long while, marveling at the color and texture time had given to that cheese, crumbling in its case.

I purchased one or two items in Matthew's store just to keep in practice, including the last of some oranges Rich had told me were available. I also discovered that the mail went out from Matthew's store, once each week, and that I was six days away from the next sending. That took care of getting any message to the outside world about the untimely presence of ice on Bennett. I hiked back up the tracks to my boat and equipment, concerned that they might already have begun a mysterious migration away from where I had left them—several people had warned me against leaving my belongings unattended around the towns of the Yukon.

Carcross: the Caribou Hotel and Matthew Watson's General Store.

However, all was untouched and intact when I reached my landing spot. I gathered my food and ensolite pad and made myself comfortable against the trunk of a fallen tree in the shade out of the hot sun, intending to enjoy a late afternoon snack while I rested and watched Rich Haupt still at work out on the ice.

Rich was definitely making progress; through my telephoto lens I could see that he was working amazingly hard and was managing to move his boat ahead, if only inches at a time. As I sat there watching I began to think of how tiresome it was going to be, carrying all of my equipment down the railroad tracks again. It would mean taking the pack frame off the back of the boat a second time, a chore which I did not relish. I realized that I was too tired to do it today, and that I would have to set up a camp for the night where I was.

My mood was losing some of its bright ebullience from the morning's travel in the face of such thoughts, so I pushed them aside and went back to thinking about Rich. I was picturing how he had worked his way down Bennett over the past few days, pulling and tugging at his boat to get it down the side of the ice sheets which stood in his way. Then, in a flash, I suddenly pictured myself doing the same thing, right here, right now. My excitement

Pulling the Quisnam around the ice, at the lower end of Bennett Lake.

wiped away my fatigue. I leaped up, ran to the boat, threw out some of the things that still remained in it, and got it back in the water. Then I gave the kayak a trial tug through the ice beside the beach. The idea, I quickly learned, was to stamp and crush the floating pans of ice by the shore, which was broad and nearly flat here, breaking them up into separate shards so that the boat might slide through them. Again there were horrible crunching sounds as the boat rode over the pieces of ice; but I could see no visible damage being done to the hull, so I continued, tossing a few things back into the boat to save my carrying them.

Very quickly I was in water up to my knees once again. Some of the pans were too thick to crumble and I had to shove and kick them out of the way, often striding into even deeper water in the process. The joy that swept over me at not having to carry the kayak down the tracks a second time was immense. It even helped me ignore the way my feet went cold, then numb, then completely without feeling. Several times I had to get out and dance up and down on the shore, to drive some sensation back into them. I was glad that it was a warm, sunny day. My excitement came through even in an entry I scribbled down in my journal: "No sleep, 20 miles of paddling, a half-mile ice-water walk, and I just *ran* back for the last load of stuff from the boat. I must be *nuts*."

Drying off, Carcross in the background.

All this time, Rich was engaged in his battle through the middle of the ice. He admitted afterwards that he was "madder than hell" when he looked up and saw me—Mr. Johnny-Come-Lately —running my boat through the ice by the shore. He also kicked himself for not thinking of doing the same thing, since he had used that very technique to start his trip. But he never stopped fighting, and finally made it through to open water and paddled over to shore to my standing ovation.

Rich handled his large, well-loaded, 15-foot Grumman aluminum canoe with a very sure touch, and he was grinning as he curved into shore. Our meeting carried an air of "Dr. Livingston, I presume" since we had both been hearing of the other's progress. I found myself very relaxed with Rich from the start, quite unlike my reaction to John and Randy at the head of the lake. Perhaps it had something to do with my having several episodes with the ice and some 25 miles of lake under my belt: I no longer felt so defensive about my abilities. It probably also involved the fact that Rich was quiet about his talents as a river traveler, showing them to me rather than telling me about them. In any case, we seemed to be friends even as we first stood there on the lake shore by Carcross, talking about the ice and chortling over our separate conquests of it.

I offered Rich a meal in the Caribou Cafe as reward for his efforts. We paddled the boats under the railroad bridge, conveniently clear of ice now, and pulled them up onto the muddy beach below the Tutshi. The cafe was closed, however, so we said goodbye to Carcross and slid rapidly down the channel connecting Bennett with Nares Lake, enjoying the sense of speed the slight current gave and the golden hues of the late evening sun. We stopped to inspect a possible campsite near the head of Nares, but it proved unacceptable because of a group of noisy people and dogs camped back in the woods. At this point I realized from my irritation and very sloppy handling of the kayak that I was by now very tired indeed. It had been a long day, and all I could think about was getting a meal and some sleep.

We continued down the lake a few more miles and finally found an excellent campsite on its lower shore. Rich ended up making dinner, producing tasty bisquits and an excellent chicken stew out of his freeze-dried supplies, and I began to feel much better as I lay warm and comfortable inside my sleeping bag spooning down this feast. We talked for a while, mostly about how happy we both were to finally be past the ice. Then I went to sleep, warm, filled with food, and pleased to have found such an agreeable companion, at least for this evening's camp.

6   Frustration and Retreat

The next morning we woke fairly early, made a quick breakfast, and loaded the boats as rapidly as possible. As I was struggling to get all my equipment down into the kayak, I noticed that Rich's canoe had at least one advantage over the Quisnam: He was able to load it very rapidly, simply dropping his equipment in, while I had to slide and carefully fit mine through the narrow cockpit opening. On the other hand, although Rich was ready to go much sooner than I was, the kayak proved to be a bit faster through the water. By the time we reached the end of Nares Lake, I was quite a ways in the lead and was the first to see around the corner into Tagish Lake. I couldn't believe what was waiting for us there. Stretching from shore to shore, and as far into the distance as I could see, was an endless, impossible field of ice. This on June 11, one day past the date when all my sources of information had assured me the entire Yukon would be absolutely clear of the cursed stuff.

I sat stunned, leaning on my paddle and drifting in the gentle current from Nares. As Rich drew closer I turned and called out, "Get ready for a shock. You're not going to believe this." And he didn't. Rich looked as though he were going to be sick. And I felt just about the same.

I left Rich to gather himself together, paddling my way up behind the ice sheet, then around its left side to the furthest point of clear shoreline I could reach. As I got closer to the ice I noted that it was quite different from that on Bennett. It lay green-white under the sun, a single, solid sheet, without the cracks or fissures that might suggest an imminent break-up. The ice was protected from the wind or any sort of wave action by a rocky bar that divided Nares Lake from Tagish. Even near the shore, the ice sheet was solid enough to stand on, and a person probably could have walked safely on it clear across the lake. It didn't look as though it would be moving anywhere in the near future.

Rich paddled listlessly to shore, and we climbed a low hill for a longer view. The ice extended for at least four miles down the lake from where we stood, unbroken, impassable, unbelievable. Rich doubted that he could make any headway chopping a passage

Nares Lake, below Carcross, looking toward our camp.

through the thick ice along the shore, since there was no place to shove the chopped-up pieces, and I knew that my rubber-hulled kayak could never take that sort of punishment. We were blocked.

After a few minutes of standing there in the warm sun, wishing fervently for a few tons of dynamite, we headed back down the hill to the boats. We sat on a rock near them for a long while, not saying much, mulling over our predicament. Then, at almost the same instant, we turned to one another to announce that the only thing left to do was to go back to Carcross and take the train from there to Whitehorse.

It was painful to contemplate eliminating a section of the trip, and I found myself wondering if I were not somehow invalidating my whole effort by taking such a shortcut. But the ice was undeniably there to stay. And I was not about to sit on Nares Lake for another ten days or two weeks or however long it would take for it to break up. Besides, once the ice finally came loose at this upper end of Tagish, logic suggested that the remains would inevitably jam up again at the mouth of the lake, just as it had on Bennett, stalling forward progress all over again. Finally, I secretly admitted that I wasn't looking forward to traveling another 50 miles over the still waters of Tagish and Marsh Lakes, with

View down Tagish Lake, with its solid jam of ice.

or without ice. My hands, showing their blisters and strangely cracked cuticles from my long day on Bennett, made me less than eager for additional long bouts of hard paddling. I was looking forward to getting a bit of help from the current on the real river beyond the lakes.

With such an excellent set of rationalizations popping into my mind, it was not long before I not only accepted the train ride to Whitehorse but actually welcomed it. Rich seemed of the same frame of mind, so we made the long pull back up Nares, paddling against the considerable current which had seemed so gentle from the other direction. We beached the boats at Carcross, below the Tutshi, and went directly to the Caribou Hotel cafe to console ourselves over hamburgers and huge pieces of homemade pie. As we sat there I was startled to look up and see John and Randy walk by. I knocked on the window, and they came clumping in in their rubber boots. They had gone part way down Bennett the day I went its length, staying on its left side rather than the side I traveled, and they were just now arriving at Carcross. When I expounded on Rich's mighty feat in blasting through the middle of the ice the day before, they only looked puzzled and then rather grandly suggested that they had had no trouble with it. Only later did I discover that yesterday's huge sheets of ice were now almost completely gone.

Randy was in and out of the cafe as we ate, busy negotiating the purchase of a set of moose horns from one of the village Indians. John and Rich talked as I sat there, and I enjoyed witnessing Rich quietly correct several of John's flat—and incorrect—statements about things on which Rich was quite knowledgeable, such as the construction of Grumman canoes. We explained about the ice ahead on Tagish, but John didn't seem to take our word for the size and difficulty of the obstacle. He and Randy soon left, radiating disparagement over our taking the train to Whitehorse. Rich watched their stroke as they paddled away and suggested that John was wise to be sitting in the back of the boat, since he was letting Randy do all the work. I saw neither one again, and I'm still curious about how long they sat behind that ice and whether they ever made it to the Bering Sea.

The train to Whitehorse did not leave until the next day, so Rich and I wandered about the Tutshi in order to kill some time. We climbed up a high, rickety ladder to get inside, studiously ignoring the Keep Out signs all about. The boat is much too huge to easily picture nosing about these now-deserted mountain lakes. It had an enormous cargo deck, two passenger decks, and above that the wheelhouse, the highest point in Carcross. The passenger decks were lined with very small, very cramped staterooms which generally held two bunks mounted against the inner walls. It is hard to imagine anyone being able to sleep in those doll-sized beds. But how magnificent it must have been riding about the lakes of the upper Yukon on this serene and gigantic paddle-wheeler. Many people must have agreed, because for years after the gold rush, there was a roaring tourist trade centered about the paddle-wheelers here at the headwaters of the Yukon.

We had finished our explorations and were settling down by our own boats to doze away the afternoon when a new diversion appeared. Rich, looking back up the channel toward Bennett Lake, suddenly leaped up, shouted "I see a floatboat," and went running up to the railway bridge to take a better look. When I caught up with Rich to find out what was happening, he explained that he thought he'd seen one of the boats of Skip Burns's Yukon tours.

When I had landed off the ferry at Skagway, I was given a welcome, and transportation, by the thin, and intense and friendly young man named Skip Burns, who owned the reddest head of hair I have ever seen. He was working at the time on an inexpensive bunk-house that he was opening in Skagway as one of the offerings

An old paddle-wheeler, the Tutshi in Carcross.

of his Yukon Safari travel firm. Another project, new this year, was a series of tours down the upper Yukon to Dawson in floatboats, substantial rubber boats which can be transported flat, then inflated for use. Rich had become acquainted with Skip during the month or two he worked in Skagway waiting to start his own trip down the Yukon, so he was expecting to see Skip and his floatboats at some point along the river.

We ran up to the bridge and after a few moments of searching, spotted the floatboat, followed by two others, blasting down on Carcross under the not-so-gentle encouragement of massive outboard motors and Skip's crew of 15-year-old boys. Skip's tour consisted of 12 paying customers and the several youngsters he employed as guides, all traveling in the three floatboats. All the boys who were helping Skip had an absolute ball during the trip, although some of his more adult customers were not so enthusiastic over the way the voyage was handled.

Skip had known of the ice on Tagish Lake, but he managed to look surprised and pained for his customers when we told him about it. He announced that we would all ride down to take a look at the ice later in the evening, for which both Rich and I were grateful. The day had been very warm, and once out of sight of the great sheet of ice it was easy to disbelieve its existence. We joked as we talked about it, but we really did want some other people to confirm that the ice was there.

Several of Skip's customers were understandably upset when they realized that the ice meant they would have to take the train back to Whitehorse—many of them had just come from there the day before. They were also unhappy about their campsite for that evening among stacks of railroad ties behind the Tutshi. Skip tried, without much success, to explain that the grassy plot he had planned on had been bulldozed away since he had last been in Carcross. Tensions were high—evidently an occupational hazard in the tour business—and it seemed prudent for Rich and me to withdraw for a while and let Skip try to sort out his problems. We helped to carry some of the tour group's equipment to the controversial campsite, then left to set up our own camp on a flat spot near the auto bridge.

After dinner Skip and those of his party who were interested picked us up for a jaunt down to the ice jam. There were two boats, and we clambered into Skip's, which carried most of the adults. It was a new experience, speeding noisily over the water in front of a churning outboard. The long cold shadows of the late evening stretched from the hills down over the lakes as we sped in the boats over the still waters. When we reached the ice there was no denying that it was indeed there; everyone in both boats agreed. We nosed about the tail end of the huge sheet for a few minutes, then turned about for the journey back to Carcross. Even though we almost ran aground several times in the shallow lake waters, the trip back took only minutes as compared to the hour or so that Rich and I had spent paddling against the current.

As I lay in my sleeping bag that evening, I realized I was eager for the train ride to Whitehorse, despite the break it represented in the trip. By now, I was associating the lakes with impossible delay and frustration. And although Bennett had been beautiful when it finally opened up before me, I wanted to be on the actual river I had come to see. I wouldn't be done with strenuous paddling on still water even beyond Whitehorse—just 30 miles below Whitehorse lay the longest lake of all, LaBerge—but LaBerge seemed a long ways away and the river at Whitehorse promised a fast current and a welcome change.

7   Onto the River and Lake LaBerge

The train with its crowd of tourists from the ferry at Skagway reached Carcross about one the next afternoon. It made a long stop there, as Rich, I, Skip Burns and his entire tour labored to load all of our equipment—including my regretfully disassembled kayak—into a baggage car and the other boats onto a flatcar. Once everything was loaded, it was restful to slump down into a stiffly upholstered seat in one of the passenger cars and watch the countryside slide rapidly past. Enough of my "kayaker" identity still clung to my grubby beard and dirty clothing to draw quite a few curious glances from the car's more respectably dressed passengers, and I felt a little out of place among normal travelers again. As we rolled along I noticed with some regret that the high mountains that stood around Bennett Lake were slipping below the horizon behind us, and that we were moving into lower, hilly country, covered with thick brush and spruce. I had liked the mountains I had been in, and I wasn't sure how agreeable the new surroundings I was traveling toward would prove to be. As the train rocked along, it passed small weed-filled ponds beside the tracks. I kept hoping that a moose might be feeding in one of them as we passed, but none were.

It was quite hot when the train reached Whitehorse, where Rich and I again helped Skip and his clients unload, being careful to keep one of Skip's young helpers watching over our own things while we worked. The people who had warned us in general about the possibility of thievery in the towns on the river had been quite specific about Whitehorse. It is a shame that such worries must plague a person even in the midst of one of the last great wildernesses on earth.

In order to safeguard our equipment, Rich and I decided to rent a room at one of the hotels by the train station near the river. We settled on the Capitol, a small hotel just a few doors away down the Whitehorse mainstreet. We were both hot and tired by the time we had all our things (excluding Rich's canoe, which we'd left with Skip's boats) stacked about the walls of our room. Spirits were revived, however, by that most blessed invention of modern society, the shower. At this point I had not had a bath since Juneau, eight days before, and had not even opened my soap container so far on the trip. The water of the upper lakes was simply too cold to make bathing or even washing an attractive prospect (or at least so I rationalized after the fact). Now, in a room again, and with the hot weather, I realized how uncomfortable and noisome I had become. The shower that afternoon in the Capitol Hotel was as refreshing and reviving as any I can remember.

Whitehorse, with its 15,000 inhabitants, is a town like those you drive through when crossing the American Midwest. We noticed, while walking around later that evening, that if one didn't look up at the spruce trees on the skyline or take notice of the endless daylight, it would be nearly impossible to tell that you were in the population center of the Yukon Territory. The character of the buildings dates back only to 1942, when construction of the Alcan Highway gave birth to today's city, and it still seems almost determinedly immature as a city, uncaring, confident and brash.

The mainstreet runs at a right angle to the river, with the train station closing its lower end. Its first block is largely given over to cheap hotels and bars, but the next few blocks contain better stores, business offices and, up several blocks on the right, a large government building and post office. There is a sense of energy and bustle about this end of the street, despite the feeling of dust which cloaks the entire town in its shallow valley and summer heat. The people here are on the move, reaching out and up for the better things in life as shown them in the Sears-like department and hardware stores. The lower end of the street seemed to counterpoint this more prosperous area away from the river. Many of the people there—mostly Indians—stood or leaned or sat with no air of meetings to make or schedules to keep. Many were also drunk and shabby. It is sad to get off a train from clear lakes and high mountain walls and be confronted with such sad derelicts, but Whitehorse is a recent meeting place between two different cultures and these were clearly the unfortunate victims of that confrontation.

The following day, June 13, was a busy one, filled with details that sent me hurrying up and down the mainstreet of Whitehorse. There was the need to check in with the Mounties, letting them know of my trip down the river so that they could establish checkpoints with their officers in Carmacks and Dawson. There was laundry to be washed and food to be purchased—enough to last most of the way to Dawson, 460 miles down river. I also spent a long time searching out a waterproof rubberized bag, which became my food bag. At one point, Rich and I helped Skip Burns get his boats over a line of pilings which stood between the train station and the river, so that he and his tour might depart before too much of the day had passed. We didn't notice it at the time, but 100 feet of good hemp rope belonging to Rich had wound up in Skip's equipment, causing us to chase after his tour all the way to Dawson.

I did not have to go far from the Capitol to do my grocery shopping. Almost directly across the street was a large department store which carried groceries in one section. I bought dried soups, crackers, margarine, peanut butter, jam (which always seems to get over everything), minute rice, boxed macaroni dinners, a can or two of stew, hash and the like for special meals, instant milk, dry cereal, sugar, candy bars and, of course, jello pudding. (I seemed to buy jello pudding at almost every place that sold it along the river, and by the end of the trip I had accumulated enough of it to make at least ten-pounds of the stuff if I had wanted.) Down the street and around the corner from the hotel, I found a shop that made salami, and I bought some at an outrageous price to store along with the margarine in the "icebox" which the near-freezing river water made of the kayak's rubber hull.

One of the most pleasant tasks of the day was looking up a man with whom I had been in correspondence several months earlier. Everyone who travels down the Yukon, it seems, must come into contact one way or another with Alan Innes-Taylor. Steve Jacobson had suggested that I write to Mr. Innes-Taylor for information at the Yukon Department of Travel and Information in Whitehorse, and his responses had been prompt and very helpful. He sent copies of old steamer maps of the river, a detailed description of the river, and several letters answering questions I asked regarding the likely date of the ice break-up. (He missed on this, but it was an unusually long winter.)

Innes-Taylor's office in the Government Building was a joy for any confirmed map-lover. The walls were papered with maps of the Yukon, and his tables and desks were littered with them. Where there were no maps on the walls, there were tall bookcases filled with volumes on the history and geography of the Yukon and its surrounding territory. As far as we could make out, Alan Innes-Taylor *is* the Department of Information. He is an old man now, over 70 I believe, but when he began talking he seemed young and vigorous indeed. He has traveled on nearly every piece of water to be found in this area of the world, including two trips down the length of the Yukon. He said that he never wanted to do the lower end of the river again because of the mosquitoes and black flies and the monotony of the countryside.

We talked about the river for quite a while, and Rich and I tried to ask intelligent questions about the country Innes-Taylor knew so well. He was very patient, only now and then asking probing questions to determine how well prepared we were for our enterprise. Apparently we passed muster, though he did take pains to give us one or two warnings about the river. We were to watch for storms on LaBerge and to be sure to keep to the right at Five Finger and Rink Rapids. He also mentioned a rather more serious matter: He didn't know for sure if the ice was entirely clear on Lake LaBerge. The talk wandered onto the subject of bears, and Innes-Taylor asked if we were carrying firearms. When we answered "No," he put our minds at ease: "Just carry a whistle. Bears don't like noise, and if you're careful, they'll never bother you. In any case, for every bear you see, ten will have seen you—and avoided you. I've never shot a bear in my life."

Indeed, Innes-Taylor seemed a most gentle outdoorsman. One summer, for example, he had lived with his family by a lake in which a moose and her calf fed each evening. By the end of the summer, through daily effort, these two shy animals had grown so used to the humans that Alan could row his daughters up to pet them as they stood feeding in the deep water. Innes-Taylor seemed quite a person. As we had already taken too much of his time, we thanked this knowledgeable old man and left him to his maps and books and fascinating memories.

Two days after arriving in Whitehorse, the day after talking with Innes-Taylor, I was sitting in the warm sun at the upper end of the old pilings that run like a forest of stumps along the water's edge below the train station. My kayak was assembled again and bobbing on the lines which held it to the shore against the pull of the green and powerful Yukon. Typically, I was waiting for Rich to return from a mission of utmost urgency in town—the buying of the last Dairy Queen coffee blizzards we would have before departure. Downriver, beyond two great paddle-wheelers rotting on the Whitehorse waterfront, lay LaBerge, Dawson and the American Yukon. How could one think of such destinations without one last coffee blizzard to steel one's nerves?

Rich came up with our stirrup-cups, and then it was time to set out on the river—the real river this time. The boat was even more heavily loaded than it had been on Bennett, because I was now carrying a good deal more food in the new waterproof bag on the back of the boat. But my equipment seemed to have gone

*Two paddle-wheelers beached at Whitehorse:
The Casca and the Whitehorse.*

through a settling process, for I now found that I had much more room in the cockpit than before. Getting into the boat was, as always, a ticklish business, especially here with the river rushing by the pilings, trying to suck the boat away from the shore. Rich asked me to wait a moment as I stood with one foot in the kayak, but I simply couldn't. I scrambled down into the loaded Quisnam, pulled the spray cover up out of the water where it always fell, snapped it down over the cockpit, and found myself whirling down the river. The first leg of the river was before me and Dawson was now the goal, 460 miles to the north.

The two paddle-wheelers rushed up and past as I clicked off three quick photos; then, swiftly, I was around the turn and away—down the river, down the Yukon. The green water weaved and dodged in little swirls and rips as the great river tempestuously raced itself down the 50-yard channel between steep cut-banks. Rolling hills covered with black spruce and thick underbrush tumbled rapidly past me. The sense of speed after the stillness of the lakes was exhilarating.

After traveling four or five miles I stopped on a sandspit below a high bank of sun-hardened sand to wait for Rich to catch up. I walked back along the river to stretch and noted one spot well away from the shore where the water was very smooth, as though it were sliding in a thin layer over something just an inch or so below the surface. My first thought was that it was a shallow point, perhaps a sand bar, and it took me a long while and several tossed stones to realize that this was a stationary boil in the water, caused by some twist of the ground far below. It began to give me some sense of the power of this great river.

Rich finally came into view, struggling to make use of his sail without much success. The winds on this stretch seemed to vary their direction almost randomly, and Rich was quite out of sorts with the effect they had on his sail. I paddled the kayak back into the current and we slid on down the river. A twist of the course brought us past the Takini, a tributary that poured so much silt into the Yukon—called the Lewes River at this point—that it was no longer possible to see the paddle blade when it dipped below the surface. The Takini added speed to the main river, however, joining it in a boiling swirling line that made the boats leap forward.

Further along, my attention was drawn by two stumps in the shadows of the shoreline shrubbery. They weren't the same color as the spruce behind and they seemed oddly shaped. Then something twitched—an ear, actually—and I realized that I was looking at the first moose, two of the huge animals, that I was to see on the trip.

When we reached the mouth of the river, where it feeds into the upper end of Lake LaBerge, it was early evening and the sun was gilding the undersides of the clouds overhead. We pulled over to take a look at the police post that the old steamer maps showed was here, actually hoping that it might still be in use and that we might be given shelter against the rain which seemed to be trying to find us. But the maps must have been speaking of history, because there was nothing there other than a cabin or two. Nevertheless, our stop was educational, for the fabled Yukon mosquito put in an appearance for the first time. There was a cloud of them on a flat above the river, looking just as gnats do when swarming, and they were voraciously hungry. We fled back into the boats, pulled away from the shore and past the pilings of some vanished structure on the right, and slid almost immediately out onto LaBerge, strange, almost haunting, under its canopy of rain clouds.

Lake LaBerge is, like Bennett, a long, narrow lake, but it is much larger and straighter—you can see its entire 31-mile length. On each side, LaBerge was hemmed in by the strangest high hills,

The first and best moose seen on the trip.

or low mountains, that I have ever seen. They were substantial hills, although not on the scale of those surrounding Bennett Lake, and they were oddly rounded and smoothed off, looking almost as though lumps of grey plastic or marshmallow had been piled up, melted, and then covered with a fine sprinkling of green—a seemingly endless forest of black spruce—which had fallen into the crevices and valleys of the melted lumps but had not covered the slopes and more vertical planes. There was an almost chilling sense of age about the whole scene, augmented this evening by the drifting clouds and the golden sun slanting past them onto the strange hills. I also had the feeling of gazing off into extraordinary distances, perhaps because of the unusual clarity of the air above the lake, or because of some perceptual trick of the land as it sloped up and away from the lake and lifted successive ranges of hills to view.

About one third of the way down the lake on the left is Richthofen Island, some three miles long; and roughly two thirds of the way down the lake, the shores press together to form a ten-mile-long narrows only two and a half miles wide. The Lewes River portion of the Yukon drains into LaBerge slightly to the right of center of its upper, southern end, and there are silt flats that extend far out into the lake, forcing one to paddle even further to the right. The old maps, however, and Innes-Taylor, recommended that we follow the left side of LaBerge, in order to avoid the winds which periodically sweep the lake, then cross back to the right along the lake's lower end to reach the outlet to the river again. Because of this advice, and the way the Lewes River enters LaBerge on the right of its upper end, Rich and I were faced with a long paddle across open water to reach the lake's left side.

As we paddled out onto the lake we were greeted by a scattering of heavy clouds with gilt sunlit fringes and black underbellies. Many of these clouds walked the land behind us on shifting stilts of rain, but the lake remained calm and smooth. By this time Rich and I were feeling the length of our day, and we were both a bit snappish. Not finding the police station, with its implications of warmth and shelter, had not helped, nor were our moods improved by the still waters and hard paddling of the lake: We had already been spoiled by the river current. We were also undoubtedly feeling the strain of dealing with one another as traveling companions. It is tiring to have to think about another person, to find out what they want to do at each juncture, especially when you are used to simply going your own way. Also, like adjoining capacitor plates, the two of you can very quickly build up an emotional charge that would never exist for a single person. So very often, if one person seems to be in a bad mood, the other eventually joins him more or less to keep him company, and you quickly end up with two very out-of-sorts people. When you are alone, there is very little reason to be in a poor mood, since you alone must suffer it. Still, despite such tensions, I think we both felt that the other's company had been a plus so far on the trip.

I was thinking of the warnings about the winds on LaBerge and the fact that we were at least a mile from the left shore toward which we were angling, when I asked Rich which point of land he wanted to head for on that shore. He answered that he planned to head for Richthofen Island, ten miles down the lake! Our exasperation with each other came into the open, as we squabbled back and forth about this—I thought it a mad idea to stay out in the middle of the lake for so long with storm clouds gathering overhead. We finally agreed to head for a point only two or three miles away down the left side of the lake.

As we labored along, apparently gaining no forward progress over the still water, I turned my head to the left and saw what I thought might be the floatboats of Skip Burns's tour. I pointed them out to Rich, who looked through his binoculars and agreed.

*A view of the Yukon below Whitehorse, my first travel
on the actual river.*

We turned to our left then, and stroked directly towards the shore.
We were no more than a hundred yards from the beach—close
enough to realize that our "floatboats" were plain wooden boats
belonging to a cabin nestled back in the trees—when a sharp wind
came racing down the lake from the south. Claps of thunder followed, and the smooth surface of the lake turned into a torrent
of whitecaps and larger rollers steaming north down the lake. It
looked uncomfortably rough for an overloaded kayak out in the
middle of the lake where we had just been, and I could only
feel grateful for the mistake in identifying a couple of rowboats
that had brought us in closer to shore.

We turned along the gently sloping shoreline to paddle down
the lake with the waves, actually surfing along with them, until
we spotted a grassy, park-like area on the shore that looked like
an excellent campsite. As we beached the boats and made a camp,
Rich was in a silent mood. We sat on a large log half-buried in
the pebbly beach well back from lapping shoreline, making our
suppers over separate fires. The clouds scudded along above us,
black and sinister where the setting sun didn't touch them, but
they never quite managed to arrange themselves to rain on us.
While we ate, I think we were both wondering if the other's com-

pany were really wanted or needed. At this point, after our first day of actually traveling on the river together, we were the furthest into the feeling of traveling *with* another person. We quickly backed away from this condition over the next several days, and ended by playing leap-frog with each other all down the river to Fort Yukon. We would stay with each other, if that's how it worked out, or would part company if one or the other felt like traveling beyond the other's stopping point. We quickly developed a very useful "to hell with him" attitude, which kept the capacitor plates of our emotions operating at a much lower, more manageable level and enabled us to travel together agreeably.

We slept that night without tents. I didn't feel like putting one up anyway, and it looked like the rain might miss us. I didn't know it at this point, but only two other times during my trip down the river would I again be free to sleep without a tent. The mosquitoes with their ravenous appetite for human blood were soon to be out in force.

I awoke at 4:30 the next morning and managed to load the boat and set off by five, leaving Rich to sleep and sail along later. I had decided that with the wind, apparently common on LaBerge in the afternoon and evening, an early start was mandatory. Rich was in less of a hurry, as he expected to take advantage of the wind with his sailing rig. I settled into the steady paddling rhythm that is necessary to cover long distances on still water, picking out a point on the shoreline ahead, making for it, then picking out the next point and so on—maintaining a fairly regular pace for the next nine hours. My efforts carried me past Richthofen Island and through the narrows, two thirds of the way down the lake. I stopped once at a small government camp on the shore opposite Richthofen Island—the unpaved Whitehorse to Dawson road swings in near the lake here. I was looking for fresh water and hoping that one of the few campers there might offer me breakfast. No breakfast was forthcoming, however, as very few of the campers were stirring at that early hour, and I was soon on my way. I stopped once again further down the lake for a rest and a stretch, but for the remainder of the morning and early afternoon I paddled continuously.

There was very little wind for the first several hours of travel, but waves, somewhat smaller than the previous night's, were still rolling to the north down the lake, and I found myself surfing down them throughout the day. The wind began to pick up as I was going through the narrows about two that afternoon, and it actually became strong enough that I could keep the boat moving

Dawn, 1 a.m. on Lake LaBerge.

along quite smartly if I chose to hold the paddle blades over my head to catch the wind, like miniature sails. My great concern as I traveled with these waves was to keep the boat lined up with them. With the boat loaded so high on the back and riding so deeply in the water, I could not allow myself to get turned sideways to the waves, as they seemed quite large enough to tip the kayak right over. As the waves passed under the boat I could feel the light wooden frame of the Quisnam flex—a very strange sensation.

The last few hundred yards through the narrow portion of the lake, lined with vertical rock walls offering no place to stop, seemed rather dicey. The wind was gaining strength, and the waves were now large rollers carrying an overlay of chop, a bad combination. I nipped around a final point of rock at last and paddled in to a low rocky beach stretching off from the lee of the rock. There I got out of the boat and made myself a snack of crackers and jam while looking about my surroundings and listening to the wind rustle the poplar leaves on the hill behind me. The day had been sunny enough, but it was beginning to cloud over now. Across the lake, heavy grey clouds obscured some of the further mountains, although my marshmallow hills were still visible as they tumbled down to the water's edge.

I had wandered to the rocky top of the hill when Rich came sailing into view and heeled over to join me on the shore. I was envious of his easy sailing before the wind—especially as I pictured him sailing happily down all the rest of the Yukon while I paddled slowly along—but in fact constant head winds prevented him from using his sail again during the trip. Rich joined me for a few more crackers, then we wandered about the beach that stretched away in a great curve, following the line of the lake as it opened out beyond the narrows. Finally, Rich hopped back into his canoe, apparently unconcerned with the increasingly stormy conditions all about us, and I loaded up to follow. We leaped off from the end of the narrows, pointing ourselves across the bay that opened on our left, heading for the next rocky point and the end of the lake beyond.

The bay was shallow for a long way out from the shore and I was grateful to sense the bottom close under me. The wind was fierce now, the waves much larger and more violent. I did not like being half a mile from shore in such conditions, and I liked it even less when the muddy color of the water marking the shallows gave way to murky blue as the bottom dropped away. The waves surged all about me, and the boat squirmed and twisted as I struggled to keep it on a proper line through them. Rich was far ahead by now, his sail driving him along over the water at great speed. As I labored to cross the bay to reach the point and its shore, Rich was already swerving by that point and heading toward the mouth of the Thirty Mile section of the Yukon, which lay on the other side of the lower end of the lake.

I slid by the first point and found myself cutting rather desperately across open water to the next. The wind and waves continued to increase, and I truly felt that I did not belong out in them. But I had it in my mind to catch up with Rich and get off the lake today. In any case, I realized that if I turned to shore now I would be putting my boat across the rollers, the very thing I was fighting against. So I kept paddling forward.

The wind was at my back, the kayak was surfing down the frothing waves as they rolled under me, and I was paddling as hard as I could to reach the next point ahead, when I realized I was creating another problem. I was moving very rapidly toward the point, but somehow I had to get around to the right of it if I did not want to be driven by the wind and water directly onto the rocks. I began cutting carefully to the right, trying to ease diagonally across the waves at as minimal an angle as possible. I just made it around the point, paddling furiously to clear the last few rocks

Flower, Lake LaBerge.

The storm coming up at the lower end of Lake LaBerge.

and bashing the paddle on the bottom in the process, and a few yards further into the next small bay I simply jumped out of the boat to hold it clear of the rocky shore.

I walked the boat toward a shallow cove which was not receiving such large breakers, feeling completely drenched and cold. I got the boat up onto the shoreline rocks out of the surging water, wondering how long the thin rubber hull could stand such treatment, then looked about, considering my predicament. Rich, sailing before the wind, had undoubtedly made it to the mouth of the Yukon, but it still lay three miles away across the end of the lake from where I stood, with heavy waves moving at right angles along every foot of that distance. I was now trapped at the lower end of LaBerge, held there by the waves. The clouds overhead were dark now, but through the storm a shaft of sunlight streamed down onto the river exit I so desperately wanted to reach. The gods seemed once again to be playing with me.

I set up my tent and gathered everything inside, then looked out as all the elements for an old-time thunderstorm began to mount over the lake. Finally, about 7:30, the show got underway. The wind was blowing so stiffly by then that birds flying forward into it were making no headway at all. Then the rain came, along with thunder and lightning, and 1 pulled back into the tent to enjoy my dry clothing and savor a delicious hot dinner of split-pea soup, tea and pudding. But, of course, now that I really wanted and needed it, the god-damned stove refused to work. My hot dinner became a cold one of jerky, crackers, peanuts and raisins. Thanks a lot, stove.

It was a wild storm, the wind whipping the tent fabric into a great cacophony of sound, and I found myself wondering again whether I would ever make it off these endless lakes and onto the river.

8 The River Again: Thirty Mile, Hootalinqua, and Big Salmon

It was 1:30 the next morning, June 16, when the silence outside the tent caused me to wake up. I poked my head out into a startling scene. It was very dark outside, with heavy clouds overhead cutting off all light except for a narrow band on the horizon above the river outlet. The lake seemed to be filled with oil, absolutely black and smooth and calm, and great banks of fog stood like ghostly draperies here and there over its surface.

I couldn't believe my good luck; the long storm had subsided to nothing, and all I had to do was load up the boat, scurry across the end of the lake, and I'd be back on the river, safely beyond the last of the Yukon's great still lakes. I was ready to set an unequaled record for the length of time it would take me to load the kayak and get underway. But just when I most wanted speed, all I got was delay and aggravation. The gods still seemed intent on playing.

I dressed quickly, putting on cut-off jeans despite the cold, because my pants were still wet from the evening before. Then I took down the tent and moved all of my equipment onto the tarp on the muddy rocks near the boat. But when I began loading—the camera case into the back of the boat, the food bag and sleeping bag onto the pack frame on the rear deck, and the clothing bag and rudder pedals into the forward section—I noticed that an inch or two of water was sloshing around the bottom of the boat, driven there the night before. Having no other way to get it out, I crouched down and sucked it up mouthful by mouthful, spitting it out over the side, until the boat was fairly dry. By the time I'd finished, the wind was beginning to come up again, and small waves lapped at the shore and rocked the kayak.

I picked up the tarp, eager to get going before the waves grew any larger, and then discovered that I had not slid the tent into the far-forward section of the boat: It was still lying hidden under a corner of the tarp. Out came the rudder pedals, out came the clothing bag, and then I found that the space for the tent was filled by a pair of tennis shoes which must have slipped back from their place in the prow during the rough sailing the day before. Using my camera tripod as a ram, I managed to shove the shoes forward out of the way. Only during this effort the attachment that fastens the camera to the tripod fell off, far up in the front of the boat. To retrieve it, I had to crawl into the forward section of the kayak, a very awkward feat with the boat afloat and shifting with the growing waves.

By the time I was finally packed and ready to go, I was wet, it was at least three, and rollers, easily as large as the ones the day before, were coming down the lake from the south. After my two-hour struggle to load, however, I was not about to take everything out again and sit trapped within sight of my goal for another day. I pushed off into the waves, barely avoiding an upset as I scrambled into the rocking boat. I need hardly add that to complete these fine beginnings of my day, my rubber boots went under the freezing water as I got in, and a clap or two of thunder came rolling across the lake to keep me company.

I could not follow the shoreline even if I had wanted to, for the waves would have worked hard to push me onto the rocks and hold me there. So I struck out directly across the end of the lake, cutting across the waves that were rolling down the lake, growing more tense as I watched the shoreline of the lake's end bay recede a quarter and then a half mile away from me. I paddled as fast as I could, to cover the three-mile distance as quickly as possible. As each wave passed under me I found that I could keep the boat reasonably upright only by leaning sharply into the wave as it approached and then in the opposite direction as it passed under me, to compensate for the roll.

That crossing was one of the most unpleasant two hours I have ever experienced, and the sound of the waves of LaBerge breaking on the shallows of the river mouth *behind* me was one of the most welcome sounds I have ever heard. The boat was drenched from waves breaking over its bow, and I was just as wet, both from the spray of the waves and the sweat of my exertions. I was very glad to be off LaBerge at last.

Once in the river mouth, I beached the boat by the wreck of an old steamer, the Casca I, which lies along the river bank like the skeleton of a gigantic sea beast. I walked around a bit, trying to get some of the damp and cramp out of my system, then got back into the Quisnam and pushed on down the river. Just around the first bend I spotted Rich's orange tent. I didn't want to wake him this early in the morning, so I slipped quietly up to his boat and used his oar to make an arrow in the sand, pointing downriver. I stood the oar upright at the tail of the arrow, to make sure Rich would see my message, then paddled quietly off. The lakes were behind me, and only river now stretched before me, all the way to the Bering Sea.

At first I was disappointed at the slowness of the current, but it quickly picked up and I made good progress down the tree-lined channel. I paddled along for an hour or so, then stopped when the sun finally peeked up over a hill and turned a green curve of the river into a warm and inviting little amphitheater. It felt good to stand in the slowly rising sun, which warmed my chilled body and made some progress in drying my wet clothing. The clouds and fog clinging to the green hills quickly burned away, my shivering stopped, and the day became delightful, perhaps as a reward for my efforts earlier that morning.

The Thirty Mile River is probably the most beautiful, intimate section of river on the entire Yukon. Its green shores are close by—no more than 25 to 50 yards apart—and the turns and straights of the river pass quickly so that there is always something new to look at. High bluffs line the river for the most part, although, occasionally, where the banks are lower, there are longer vistas of the high hills beyond, cloaked in endless forests of black spruce. Poplars and willows and grassy meadows ornament the water's edge.

Innes-Taylor had reported that many varieties of animals might be seen along this stretch of river, but this early morning I saw only one or two surprisingly large bald eagles drifting like dark gliders along the river's shores. But lack of game did not reduce the pleasure of simply sliding down the river. So tranquil was the setting that on straight stretches I found myself nodding asleep perhaps six or seven times. The roar of water passing through matted piles of trees or rushing over submerged rocks soon put a stop to these slumbers, however. I found that going from excellent sleep to instant strenuous paddling away from danger was just too much of a strain.

The Thirty Mile River runs generally north from LaBerge for about 20 miles, then turns to the east to meet the Teslin River at Hootalinqua, site of an old North West Mounted Police post. I was surprised how quickly I covered the miles from LaBerge to the NWMP post, for I reached the post after only six or seven hours of travel, my progress greatly aided by the speed of the river's current. Hootalinqua means "Where Two Big Waters Meet," a very apt description; for the Teslin, which joins the Thirty Mile River at the bottom of a deep fold in the surrounding high green hills, was broad, heavy with brown silt, and littered with floating trees, shrubs and other debris. It was obviously at full flood. At

The cut-banks of the Thirty Mile River.

the first sight of the debris on the river, I thought that I had stumbled onto the perfect photo of a moose swimming the river before me. I carefully crept up behind, camera at the ready, only to discover that my moose was a very moose-like stump starting its journey down the Yukon.

I paddled over to the Hootalinqua site on the left shore, very pleased with the warm noon sun streaming down onto my shoulders. It took only a moment to get everything out of the boat and spread to the sun on the grassy slope leading from the shore to the three ruined cabins that I believe served as a Mounty monitoring station for the thousands of boats that came down the river in 1898. A fourth building, a shack still used by Water Survey patrols in the winters, had a sign inside which gave its history and invited anyone who needed to to use the cabin, admonishing them only to replace all used firewood and kindling when they finished with it. There was also a guestbook to sign, and some of the entries made fascinating reading—especially those written by people who had somehow reached this lonely spot during the winter. One of these spoke of sighting a pack of wolves just south of the small cabin.

I stayed in Hootalinqua for a couple of hours, savoring the sun, the quiet, the flowing rivers and the sense of history of the place.

A few clouds gave character to the blue sky, but for the most part the sun poured down unhindered, a wonderful change after the earlier morning's biting cold. A few mosquitoes buzzed about to keep the setting from being absolutely perfect, but even they could do little to damage my cheerful mood. It was great to be off those lakes and, finally, to be embarked on the flowing Yukon at last.

I had to force myself to pack my dry belongings back into the boat and set off again down the river. A few hundred yards from Hootalinqua, I passed an island where paddle-wheelers were built. The steamer Evelyn still sits on the ways there, waiting sadly for a return of the bustle and activity which has vanished from the river forever. After the entrance of the Teslin, the Yukon becomes a bigger concern—a much, much bigger concern. It broadens to a good quarter of a mile wide, and what were previously only small spots of roiling water now become large enough to grab the kayak and turn it about, giving a person riding the river's back some sense of the power under him.

As I flew along at up to ten miles an hour, now and again I would hear ahead the scary sound of what could only be an uncharted waterfall across the river, or perhaps an express train blasting along the shore. Eventually, meeting no waterfall or train, I realized that the sound was simply the river being pinched by some lump or rib of solid rock or a drowned tree or root, causing the water to roar past the obstruction like a rocket launching.

Perhaps most indicative of the power of the river—and of how very high it was as I raced down its surface—was the fact that all of the islands I passed had bow waves! The water ripped by these islands with such speed and energy that every one of them threw up a wave at its upper end, just as though they were a fleet of cruisers forcing their way upstream through the river's current. I was to meet several people along the river who confirmed that they had never seen its waters so high before. The high water was both good and bad for me: It was great for pace and distance, but it presented a problem when it came time to find a campsite. The best place to camp on the river, cool and free from mosquitoes, is on the upper end of an island, on the pleasant flat sandbars which form there. Now those pleasant bars were under two or three feet of water, and camping sites proved very hard to find all down the river.

The water presented a strange picture, stretching from shore to shore—almost from tree root to tree root—across the river. If it had been another few inches higher, many of the river's islands

The remains of Hootalinqua.

would have been entirely under water. Nevertheless, it was a
delight to simply drift down this massive new river after my morning
exertions, letting its incredible power carry me along, spinning
and twisting in the boil spots which constantly appeared and disappeared. Why not drift, when the river offered such speed? Paddling
seemed almost an affront to its might.

I pulled over to a sand spit at about five o'clock, to nap for
20 minutes or so, hoping to recover some of the energy I could
feel waning as the day's hours grew longer. As I walked about
to stretch before lying down, I discovered I was sharing the spit
with a pair of grumbling ducks who resented my intrusion. They
waddled about, complaining about my presence, the male ruffling
his stunning black and white feathers with great indignation. They
were clearly asking me to leave them be, which I did by moving
away. The sun was warm on my back as I lay on the tarp, and
I soon drifted off. There are few things so pleasant as being free
to stretch out in some warm, out of the way place at a time of
your choosing, and then fall slowly asleep.

I awoke just in time to see Rich go racing past. I let out a
blast on my newly purchased bear whistle to let him know I was
there, then quickly got back into the kayak—rather too quick-

ly—and pushed off from the island. Immediately I had to beat a hasty and difficult retreat back against the current; one of my rudder lines had come undone, and I couldn't control the boat without it. I was learning a lesson that was to be repeated one or two times further down the river: Make sure *everything* is ready before you set out, because it is difficult, if not outright impossible, to turn back once the current has a hold on you.

It took me a long while to catch up with Rich, even though he was just drifting and I was paddling vigorously. The swift current had carried him far down the river during the few minutes I was concerned with the rudder wire. Rich was "just around the bend," but after the entrance of the Teslin, as I have noted, the entire scale of the river became much grander. On the smaller river the view down a straight stretch might cover as much as a quarter or half a mile. But here, a similar view from one bend to another might cover two or three miles. This scale was to continue and increase all down the Yukon. Saying that some destination lay "three bends away" might mean that it was 20 miles away.

Rich seemed pleased to have my company again, as was I to have his after the long day. He admitted that he had been a little miffed at discovering that I had passed by his tent without awakening him, perhaps with some thought that I was trying to be first down the river. He was quite mollified, however, when he learned of the early hour of my passing. We rode the river, now hanging onto each other's gunnels, now drifting down the river a quarter of a mile apart. When we floated side by side we found ourselves constantly talking about the size of the river under us. Neither of us could get over its dramatic increase in scale. When the shadows of the shoreline trees were quite long across the river and we were both beginning to think about dinner and rest, we came to the point where the Yukon is joined by the Big Salmon River, which flows out of a mountain range of the same name, draining some 2,000 square miles before it joins the Yukon.

We were hugging the bank as we approached the juncture, because we wanted a close look at the village of Big Salmon, located on the lower right shore. As we came around the point of land between the Yukon and the Big Salmon rivers, we saw not only the old trading post but also a Klepper Double down on the shore and what looked like a group of Indians sitting in front of the cabins of the village with several white men. There were two or three blue tents standing among the four or five buildings of Big Salmon, and clothing and equipment was strewn about everywhere.

Rich and I almost simultaneously decided that we wanted to try and stop at this unexpected and interesting congregation.

We began paddling toward the village, at first rather casually, but then, as we hit the downstream force of the Big Salmon, we were forced to paddle as fast and furiously as we could. The current was carrying us downstream nearly as fast as we were moving across it toward the shore. Someone from the village came running down to the shore just as I began to wonder if it was all worth it. He was yelling "Keep coming, you can make it" at the top of his lungs, so I tried even harder, feeling that my paddle was close to breaking as it flexed and bent in my grip. Despite my efforts, I could only watch helplessly as the open space of the village passed by, to be replaced by thick green shrubbery extending down the shore and into the water. Fifty yards below the village I crashed into the plants and only by grabbing an armful of branches managed to stop the boat from shooting right out again on the surging current. Rich, who had started his effort further up the river, accelerated his more massive canoe with great skill and reached the shore considerably closer to our intended goal.

Wondering what the villagers were thinking of my approach, I held fast to the plants, got one foot out of the boat and onto the edge of the bank, and pulled myself upright with one hand tugging against the nose of the cockpit coaming. I should say *almost* pulled myself upright: The bank did not shelve out at any sort of an angle under the water but instead went three feet straight down—and I went right down with it, half sitting in the boat, half standing in the freezing water. I scrambled up out of the water, tied the boat to the shore bushes, then squished my way back through the brush on the bank to meet the inhabitants of Big Salmon.

All these "inhabitants" proved to be travelers. None of them were either Indians or traders, and the group was by far the most hang-loose of any I met on the river. The six men who composed it were all recent graduates of Eastern universities who had hit on the wild idea of celebrating the completion of their academic efforts by going down the Yukon from Whitehorse to the Bering Sea in three grossly overloaded Klepper Double kayaks.

With generous hospitality, these six travelers offered us coffee and insisted that we share their dinner, a truly nasty dehydrated meatloaf concoction which they had bought at bargain rates as the staple of their diet for their entire voyage. Having been on the river for only a week or two at this point, they nonetheless could barely stand the sight of their only substantial food for the duration of their trip to the Bering Sea.

As we stood around talking, Rich and I were at first somewhat restrained with these strangers, but their hospitality was so easy and open and their personalities so delightfully mad that we quickly relaxed. All of our new acquaintances seemed to have cameras of one sort or another, all except one who pointedly announced that he had no camera and was proud of it. I was also carrying my camera and long lens, and as Yukon Madness seemed rampant that evening, I found myself in a western-style photographic shoot-out with one of the six, who exuded a slightly sinister air from under his black cowboy hat. His small automatic camera was definitely the faster, but my lens was of such a much larger caliber that I feel I won the encounter hands down.

Rich and I finished eating the nearly inedible remains of their supper, wondering how they could endure such a fate. We then thanked them and announced that we would be going on down the river: The mosquitoes here were simply unacceptable—the six had nearly filled an old tobacco can with bodies of the little monsters they had slaughtered during the evening—and, in any case, the men and their mass of equipment had occupied virtually every clear space in Big Salmon. Our hosts asked us to tell the Mounties in Carmacks that they would be a little longer getting there than originally expected; their two or three hours of drifting lazily down the river each day, roped together like a giant three-petaled flower, were not carrying them along quite as fast as expected. We thanked our hosts again, wished them encouragement in the face of their culinary misfortune, and took off. I hope they made their final destination successfully.

It was late by then, and both Rich and I wanted to find a place to camp as quickly as possible. I had been up for 19 hours, traveling for 17, and had covered over 70 miles from my storm-blown camp on LaBerge. But another six or eight miles of river had to pass before we spotted a gravel spit trailing off from the lower end of a nearly submerged island: The river was so high most of the campsites were underwater. Our gravel spit was very low, but it seemed acceptable. We quickly beached, unloaded our things and set up a camp. The mosquitoes were bearable here, so we both trusted to repellent instead of tents to get us through the evening unscathed. It had proved to be an excellent first day beyond the last of the Yukon's lakes, the way a day on the Yukon in a kayak ought to be.

9　Little Salmon, Carmacks, Five Finger Rapids, and Minto

June 17 dawned warm and clear, and I spent a leisurely two hours breakfasting and preparing the boat and equipment for another day's travel. Rich, as usual, was ready to go much sooner than I because of the ease with which his canoe was loaded. He shoved off a few minutes before me, and I had my early morning exercise catching up with him.

Our morning effort covered roughly 25 miles, from the gravel bar to the town of Little Salmon. The country was far more open than it had been on the Thirty Mile section of river, and the river itself was much bigger since the entrance of the Teslin tributary. The field of view was on a vast scale, with open vistas stretching away through the nearby rolling hills to larger green mountains beyond. By this time I was firmly relying on my topological maps to tell me where I was, as the old steamer maps had proved themselves wildly, comically inaccurate. One, which I had purchased in a Whitehorse store, informed the reader that after an eight-mile advance down the river toward Dawson, he had in fact retreated a distance of 25 miles, an interesting navigational achievement. The scales on the steamer maps also varied wildly, with two equal lengths of the river standing for five miles in one case, ten or fifteen in another. I wonder how the steamers managed to survive such mapping.

My topo maps, on the other hand, were amazingly accurate, despite the fact that they had been made from photos taken as long ago as 1949. Such accuracy impresses on one the timelessness of a great river's existence; 25 years is the merest flash in time for a river existing on geologic time. A few changes were notable, of course. Stewart Island, for example, a day's travel above Dawson, loses up to 30 feet of land a year to the river and is fast disappearing, and the Yukon Flats are virtually impossible to map accurately over any length of time.

My topo maps told us that we were near Little Salmon around lunchtime. We slid closer to shore and began peering up through the trees and brush, searching for some sort of indication of the town. Finally, we saw some buildings, and I made another of my graceful landings: My technique was to bash right into the growth on the shore's edge and grab hold of something before I shot back out into the current again.

We overshot the buildings getting to shore and had to climb up through thick underbrush and a dense network of fallen poplar trees. At last we reached the structures we had seen from the river and briefly wondered if we had stumbled into a village built for pygmies. We were not standing in the town of Little Salmon, but in its cemetery, and we were surrounded by Indian spirit houses and slightly more familiar looking fenced-in graves bearing the distinctive Anglican cross. There were perhaps 15 or 20 of the little buildings stretching along a path through the thick woods. Each house was quite carefully constructed, with windows and even a doorway here and there, but everything was in a miniature scale, standing three or four feet high. The houses covered grave mounds, and I presume that they were built to give the dead an acceptable resting place. Rich and I felt like two Gullivers moving about a Yukon Lilliputia.

In one of the houses, the most intricately constructed of the lot, there was an old, battered suitcase. We opened it and learned that the small house was Miss Ann Joseph's final residence. The suitcase contained letters and bits of clothing and several photographs nearly blank with age. I carefully replaced the suitcase and its contents, wondering if we had committed some form of desecration by handling the materials. I decided that the opposite was probably more correct. The memory of Miss Ann Joseph can exist for strangers only through the little house and the objects in that suitcase, and by looking at them, we prolonged her presence in this world. And now you too know of Miss Ann Joseph.

Rich and I walked along the path leading from the cemetery, looking for the full-sized town of Little Salmon, and found that it was just a larger-sized village of spirits. It lay in a large grassy meadow fronting the river, and all that remains of the town is the sturdy log and sod Anglican church, an abandoned cabin or two, a rusted truck, and a battered, flat-bottomed, blunt-nosed 30-foot riverboat pulled up on the shore. The construction of highways, and the consequent shift of commerce away from the river, had emptied Little Salmon, along with all the other Indian villages between Whitehorse and Carmacks, and now it was as empty and silent as the graveyard which stood nearby.

We returned to the boats and paddled out onto the current. The steamer maps stated that we were 42 miles from Carmacks, and the topo maps seemed to agree, so we made the town our next destination. After having devoted myself to paddling through

Spirit houses in the Little Salmon Indian graveyard.

much of the morning, I felt that a rest was in order, so I spent the early part of the afternoon drifting and reading an Andre Norton sci-fi book I had found in Whitehorse.

It was very pleasant, simply coasting along on the current, dipping in and out of a book. I looked up frequently to check my effortless forward progress, admiring each new scene the river had provided while I was reading. At times, I found myself staring into slanting rock striations in a nearby wall, layers of an ancient geologic history; at other moments, I was gazing into the distance, over the ever-present dark-green carpeting of black spruce toward the hills and mountains that roll off into the distance, all under a great blue canopy graced with fluffy white clouds. I experienced a continual, inescapable sense of the huge size and extent of this nearly empty wilderness. There is so much uninhabited space up here, and it has stood empty and waiting for so very long—for ages before man first intruded over the Bering land bridge. One brief flood of human numbers has poured through it, during the rush toward Dawson and gold, and now the land is empty again, waiting for who knows what.

As the afternoon grew into evening, the clear sky gave way to clouds that grew darker and darker. And with the clouds came wind, sweeping up the river, ending my heedless drifting. It constantly fought to turn the kayak back to front and slowed progress so much that I could sit there and watch bits of wood and debris on the water's surface drift speedily by me. By the time the bridge at Carmacks came into view, I was hunched far forward, trying to reduce my wind resistance and paddling furiously to keep control of the boat. Just before Carmacks the river follows a right-hand curve that continues on past the town, and as I rounded this curve, fighting the wind and the waves it kicked up, I could see Carmacks through the struts of the bridge, on the left bank of the river. I passed under the bridge on the right and belatedly realized that I would have to paddle like a maniac if I meant to reach the town before the river carried me far beyond it: It was the strain of Big Salmon all over again, only extended over a much longer distance.

Nothing like proper permanent docks or breakwaters can be built for the towns along the Yukon, because the ice would simply grind and scour them away each spring. What docks there are are built on pontoons, shoved into the water each spring when the ice clears and pulled up on shore each fall. As the town raced by, or rather as I churned past on the eight to ten mile-an-hour current, paddling for shore with all my might, I spotted such a dock and headed for it. It was the only one extending into the water in front of the town, and the shore beyond looked steep and difficult for any sort of a stop: If I missed the dock, I pretty well missed Carmacks.

In a current such as the one speeding along the shoreline of Carmacks, my problem changed abruptly from reaching the goal of the temporary dock to that of avoiding a crash into it: I was moving quite fast, and the dock was a solid stationary object directly ahead in the current. I came charging down on the dock, pushed my right foot far forward on the rudder pedal for a hard right turn, backpaddled on the right to swing broadside to the upper edge of the dock, and managed to fend it off with my arms before crunching into it. I then hand-walked my way around to the lower side of the dock and scrambled out, while holding tight to the kayak to keep the current from carrying it off. Rich was only a few hundred yards behind and, with an equally desperate effort, managed to reach the same dock. (I was continually amazed at how fast Rich could move his canoe when he had to. My kayak was faster, and my double blade gave me two strokes to his one; but when he put his mind to it, and his back, he could really move that canoe.)

The bridge at Carmacks.

The dock held a prominent sign informing us that it was the property of the Forest Service and that anyone not connected with that organization was definitely not welcome on its surface. I walked to the Forestry building just across the road, poked my head in the door of a workroom, and in my most friendly tone informed the two men sitting there "We've just come down the river, and our boats are tied up at your dock." Before I even got to voice my request that we be allowed to stay there, the response came: "Well, move them!" The man's manner wasn't even remotely friendly, although he did explain, curtly, that fire-fighting amphibious planes were using the dock to pick up equipment and that he didn't want them getting tangled up in anybody's kayak or canoe. I suggested that we could move the boats out of the way, but he insisted that we move them completely away.

I walked back to the dock and told Rich, who had a few unkind words for the Forest Service. We were both tired from a long day, the constant afternoon wind, and the hard pull across the river. Now we had to move the boats, and it was a bit questionable where we could move them to. We searched the steep bank ahead—there was no going back against the current here—and finally spotted a dock still pulled up on the bank, but with one edge sticking down into the water. We would have to make for that, some 200 feet below us.

Rich made the new dock easily, but I had a bit of a problem even leaving the first dock. The kayak was more than three feet below the level of the Forest Service dock, with the current fighting to sweep it away. Since I would be unable to reach the line once I was inside the Quisnam, I had to untie the kayak before I got in; but once it was untied it was nearly impossible to hold still against the river, since my only way of holding it beside the dock was with my feet in the cockpit. I found no difficulty whatsoever in picturing myself floundering in the water while the kayak headed off alone for Dawson. There was nothing else for it, however, so at last I leapt down into the kayak, successfully. I was still trying to arrange things to begin paddling when Rich leaned out from the second dock and caught me as the current carried me by.

We tied up at this second dock and walked up to check in with the RCMP office. A very pleasant young man, out of uniform, talked with us briefly about the river. He said that it was higher than anyone in Carmacks could remember and that it was driving past at a good seven or eight knots—in other words, at nine or ten miles an hour. He checked us off the list of travelers coming down the river from Whitehorse and recorded the message we carried from the six intrepid kayakers of Big Salmon.

Earlier that afternoon, as we had drifted together down the twists and turns of the giant river, Rich and I had talked at length about great meals we had enjoyed in the past, putting as much intensity into the details of these memories as though we had been months out on some foodless desert. This often seems to happen, I've discovered, when you are out camping—You get the miserable munchies of the mind despite having perfectly good and filling food for the body. As a result of our afternoon conversation we practically crawled into the single cafe of Carmacks, half starved, and we both consumed meals fit for men rescued from a desert isle—mine consisted of salad, steak and eggs, pie a la mode, and two strawberry milkshakes. The tariff for this feast came to over $5, reflecting the inflated food prices of the far north, but it was worth it. The cafe served as the dining room for Carmacks's hotel, and as we ate we were entertained by the jocular bantering between the young white and older Indian fire-fighters who stay there when they are not out dousing flames.

After dinner we stocked up on candy bars—you never can tell when you might find yourself on the verge of starvation again—and

Camp and an evening ritual, below Carmacks.

got back into our boats, intending to go downriver from Carmacks for a mile or two to set up camp for the night. The river below Carmacks swings through four alternating horseshoe bends, however, and we had to navigate each one, a distance of about eight miles, before I finally spotted a clearing and what looked like the remains of a fishing camp set into the thick shoreline foliage of an island we were passing. The air was cold—the sun had disappeared behind the surrounding hills—and we were relieved to find this spot.

The First Airborne Mosquito Brigade, Carmacks Division, was out in force that night and encouraged me to raise and enter my tent in record time. The next several minutes were spent watching the intricate maneuvers of the First as its members wheeled and dived and buzzed at the tent, daring me to come back out for battle. I declined, however, meticulously dispatched all the little devils that had entered the tent with me, and was soon asleep. The final note in my diary for this day pointed out that I had managed to get through the whole day of roughly 70 miles without getting wet, a major technical breakthrough.

The next morning the sky was overcast and bleak, so both Rich and I simply remained in our tents for several hours, reading and dozing. We finally got moving about noon, fought off the mosquitoes for our possessions, and were heading down the grey river toward our adventure for the day, Five Finger Rapids. Now that a dam has flooded Miles Canyon above Whitehorse, these are the only rapids worthy of the name that remain on the river. Everyone we talked with about the river stressed that we should go through the rapids on the right side, as though they were at least worthy of some careful attention. So, when we reached Five Finger Coal Mine under a grey sky just on the verge of rain, we pulled over to the side to batten down our boats and minds for the confrontation, spending only a little time exploring the remains of a rickety wooden framework which marks the site.

I didn't notice it at the time, but in getting out of the boat, or back in, I managed to lose the gloves I had been wearing since Whitehorse, my first loss of the trip. However, I didn't even notice that my hands were strangely bare—my mind was too occupied with Five Finger Rapids just ahead. At least Five Finger Rapids were supposed to be just ahead. Actually, they were at least a mile or so from the mine, and by the time we finally came into sight of the rapids, all my readiness and "up for it" state of mind had dissolved into something nearer casual disdain. I pulled over and held to the bank on the right side, waiting for Rich to catch up and pass, since he had done a lot of white water running in canoes in New England and the South. That morning he had talked briefly about "finding a line" through the rapids and about letting them "carry you through." I had nodded knowingly to all this, not understanding a thing. Since I had never even seen white water from a boat before, Rich's going first seemed like an excellent idea.

Five Finger Rapids exist because of four house-sized rock "hoodoos" that stand in a chain across the river. These flowerpot islands of stone, unique on the Yukon, divide the river into five narrow, 30- or 40-foot channels. As I looked ahead at them, sliding along behind Rich, all I could see was a smooth curl of water between the rocks, especially on the right. This didn't look like any sort of a big deal at all. I even said as much to Rich, as he paddled tentatively along ahead of me toward the space between the first rock and the right bank.

Just as I finished voicing my rash opinion, Rich's canoe was yanked in a swirling half-circle to the right by an eddy of water squeezing to get through the rocky barricade ahead. A moment later I was yanked to the left. I paddled sharply to straighten myself out and found that *I* was now leading our little procession.

The Hoodoos above Five Finger Rapids.

We were under the rocky wall which looms over the rapids on the right, along which you can still see remains of the ropes and cables that were used to winch steamers up through these rapids when the big boats were in common use on the river. I was just able to see over the smooth blue line of water between the wall and the rock on the left, when Rich called out softly, "Good luck."

And my God but how I wanted that good luck!Beyond and below the smooth curl of water toward which I was plunging, the river seemed to explode into a field of white-topped haystacks, monumentally huge great geysers shooting their frothy tops up into the sky. Couldn't I just stop a while and reconsider the whole thing? No. Down over the center of the curl I went, plunging straight into the haystacks. They probably were not much over three or four feet high, if even that, but to my inexperienced eyes they seemed gigantic beyond belief. The Quisnam flexed up and down, bouncing straight through them, until one wave smashed into the side, drenching me through the spray cover and twisting the boat around. A single stroke set me back straight, and a moment later I was through, riding in a high chop which seemed smooth as silk after what had gone before. I pulled about to watch Rich come through.

Rich bailing, after the rapids at Five Fingers.

He was close behind me, but he seemed to be having more trouble than I had. His canoe was turned sideways a bit and almost hidden in the waves. He emerged a moment later and called for me to get a photo as he began bailing operations: One of the waves had come in over the front of his canoe, dumping at least three inches of water into its bottom, and Rich felt lucky that he had managed to avoid further difficulties with the next waves. He allowed as how these rapids were the biggest he had ever gone through. I didn't inform him that they were the *first* I'd ever experienced.

Undoubtedly the river, as high as it was, made these rapids more spectacular than usual. Most knowledgeable people to whom I've mentioned them felt that they were fairly tame, but I just don't think that they were. I must admit that from a kayak even a ripple looks like a wave, and a real wave looks like a veritable *tsunami*. But I am sure that I was looking *up* at the waves in Five Finger, an experience I was not eager to repeat, especially with the boat as loaded down as it was.

For a moment, though, four or five miles further down the river, it looked as if the experience was to be repeated again. Rink Rapids had been a formidable obstacle for the steamers during

Rink Rapids.

their heyday, and we were warned to avoid going through them in the middle or on the left because of the dangerous hulks of steamers that had not made it. However, a channel was blasted around the rapids on the right years ago, and Rink Rapids no longer pose a real obstacle to boat travel. Still, when you come onto these rapids around a right-hand turn, and the first view you see is of their turbulent left-hand portion, you can't help thinking "Here we go again." But a moment later, the relatively calm right-hand passage swings into view around the curve, and you paddle comfortably by.

With the two sets of rapids behind, I could feel the adrenalin finish its work and the resulting tiredness creep into my body. Five Finger was a shock, as was the first view of Rink Rapids, but having gotten through both of them successfully, I thought that I could see how white water kayaking might be fun—with experience and a less heavily-loaded boat. I wonder what my attitude would have been had I not been so fortunate as to experience "beginner's luck" on my first ride through rapids.

We stopped briefly below Rink Rapids to readjust our boats and stretch, and at this stop I made a discovery which, while simple, was to improve the rest of the trip down the river. I'd been experiencing an irritating soreness of my lower back after sitting or paddling in the boat for any length of time. The seat in a Klepper is formed by a board that clips onto the flat keel and a small, nearly round backrest on a rod that runs between the sides of the cockpit coaming. No matter how you sit or scrunch or twist or turn, nothing seems to make that seat supportive and comfortable for long periods of time. But on that narrow wind-swept shore, with a light rain just beginning to sprinkle down, I had a stroke of genius. I blew up the small cushion I'd been using as a pillow at night and strapped it over the backrest. The slight give of the air inside must have let the blood circulate more easily, or some such thing, because the next few hours were the most comfortable I spent in the boat, reading and drifting and enjoying the calm after the rapids.

Late that afternoon, having traveled out from under the brief light rain, we reached the town of Minto and made camp for the night. The town was deserted in 1954 because of unexplained murders (sorry, that's all I know about it), but I believe that a new town, or at least a few residences now exist a few miles south of the old townsite: Near the abandoned town, we saw an Indian couple and their children, apparently picnicking by the water at the end of a dirt road. They stood and looked at us as though we were the unknown murderers returned, and a few minutes later we could hear them take off up the road in an ancient car. We drifted for a short distance further and pulled out on a bulldozed flat obviously used as the boat-landing area for the village. Another of the big river boats was lying there on the flat, like a beached whale, its wood dry and splintering.

The mosquitoes were so bad here that Rich and I both pulled out the headnets we were carrying. Mine was a simple one of netting that covered my head and neck, while his was a magnificent affair, hanging to his waist, that his sister-in-law had made him. Both headnets proved to be invaluable for keeping one's sanity throughout the rest of the trip, as the whine and buzz of mosquitoes about your face is almost worse than their constant bites. We both set up our tents while wearing these beautiful contraptions, looking like men from Mars.

Our campsite lay just below a flat open field, about a quarter of a mile long, which was dotted with the remaining cabins of old Minto. There was also a very well-built church and a multi-roomed store with a musty two-roomed cellar. I wandered about, then turned back toward the tents and a dinner of salami and crackers, canned beef stew, orange drink, and that staple food

Sunset on the Yukon, at Minto.

for all wilderness travelers, "gorp"—peanuts and raisins. (Classic gorp also contains chocolate M&Ms.) It was an interesting experience eating inside the mosquito helmet. Every now and then I would forget to raise it from my mouth before taking a spoonful of food, with somewhat messy results. But the netting was absolutely necessary, else the mosquitoes would surely have accomplished another of those unsolved murders.

10   Fort Selkirk, Coffee Creek, the Camerons, and Two Moose

Early on the morning of June 19, I learned one of the drawbacks to sleeping in a tent: When the sun hit my tent's orange walls, they absorbed the heat and quickly made the interior more like an oven than a sleeping area. There was nothing for it but to get up, long before I really wanted to, and brave the needle-nosed mosquitoes waiting eagerly for blood outside. My headnet and liberal amounts of repellent proved relatively equal to the challenge, however, so I decided to take another walk around the old buildings of Minto to photograph them.

I carried my camera and tripod up to the first group of buildings on the flat above our camp and had wandered through several of them when I noticed that the clamp on the top of the tripod was missing. This was the same clamp that had caused so much difficulty when it fell into the forward compartment of the boat on Lake LaBerge. I was desolate. The loss of the clamp made the tripod useless: Without it the camera could not be attached.

I retraced my steps through the empty houses of Minto and back to the tents, but I knew the search was hopeless. This was the second item, along with the gloves left at Five Finger Mine, that I had lost in the past two days. Whenever you undertake any sort of a trip in which you travel under your own power, you carry with you just those things you will need, and you can afford to lose none of them. Yet I'd managed to lose two important pieces of equipment in two days! It did not make me very happy.

Sitting near my tent, listening to Rich waking in the heat of his, I suddenly had one of those flashes that forces one to wonder about the possibilities of ESP. I'd been using the tripod to arrange equipment in the end of the boat the night before. Could the clamp have dropped off again as it had on LaBerge, without my noticing it? Indeed it had. There it was, lying by itself way up in the bow of the kayak. I felt as though I had discovered a diamond or golden nugget. The "lose-its" are one of the worst ailments to suffer from while traveling, and it is incredibly pleasing, under such conditions, to find something you think you have lost.

Out on the river an hour or so later, I was still happy about my find despite the headwind that whistled past me, slowing progress and forcing me to paddle constantly in order to keep the

Approaching Fort Selkirk.

boat facing into the wind. The day was bright and warm, and the clouds in the sky were white and fluffy rather than grey and mean as they had been the day before. By three that afternoon we had covered the 20 miles to the high basalt cliffs and higher mesa that mark the entrance of the Pelly River, the fifth largest tributary of the Yukon. A few minutes later, the first buildings of the town of Fort Selkirk appeared on a long flat bluff which fronts the left shore of the river for three or four miles.

Fort Selkirk—That name, for no real reason, carried for me the most impact of the many famous names I had read on my Yukon maps before setting out on this voyage. The name seemed to reach back beyond the age of the gold seekers, to an earlier time when the only white men in all the Northwest were intrepid Mounties and lonely trappers and traders exploring the land for the Hudson's Bay Company. And, in fact, Fort Selkirk does have a history to match this impression. It dates back to June 16, 1843, when Robert Campbell, in the employ of the H.B.C., drifted with three companions out of the mouth of the Pelly and first set eyes on the broad Yukon River. He returned five years later and set up a trading post for the company on an island in the mouth of

Rear of the general store in Fort Selkirk.

the Pelly River. The post flourished, and Campbell's explorations made the surrounding territory "known" to whitemen: One of his trips down the river reached Fort Yukon, and for the first time the Hudson's Bay Company became aware that its two outposts were located on the same river.

On August 21, 1852, Campbell's post was wrecked by the coastal Chilkat Indians, who had previously held a monopoly on trade with the upper Yukon from the coast. Campbell responded in a way that must have been commonplace with these heroic explorers of the unknown north but seems fantastic today: He walked from Selkirk to Minnesota, in the dead of winter, to board a train to Montreal, there to ask the governor of the Hudson's Bay Company to grant him permission to rebuild Selkirk. His request was denied, and he never returned to what he termed "the most splendid river."

The Fort Selkirk area was not visited again by whitemen for the next 16 years, until two men working for Western Union reached the area. They were part of an abortive effort to run a telegraph line to Europe by way of Alaska and Russia, an idea conceived and backed by men who were certain the trans-Atlantic cable was an impossibility. One of these men was Mike LaBerge, whose

Winter transportation, Fort Selkirk.

name, or some variation on it (LeBarge, LaBarge or LeBerge), stands on the Yukon's longest lake. LaBerge and his companion found the fort burned and deserted.

In 1892 Fort Selkirk was reborn on the flat bluff across the river from the island where Campbell had created his outpost. This time the force behind its construction was not worldly commerce but concern for the spirit: Its new role was that of a mission for the Indians. In 1898 Fort Selkirk acquired further inhabitants when it was designated the headquarters for the Yukon Field Force, the peace-keepers in the area during the gold rush.

Now Fort Selkirk is nearly deserted again, and has been since the early fifties. Rich and I tied up on the shore and climbed the steep bank, to take a closer look at the 15 or 20 weathered frame buildings that stretched in a rough line away from us along the bluff, ending in a church spire and the larger buildings of the town center a quarter of a mile away. We began to walk along the high bank, but we had not gone very far before a team of huskies, staked out for the summer behind a small log cabin on our left, yowled an alert. The cabin door flew open, and a young Indian girl, dressed in jeans and a blue shirt, came running out to ask us to sign a notebook she was carrying.

The girl's name was Lois Roberts, daughter of Danny Roberts, the self-appointed caretaker of Fort Selkirk. She was 17-years-old, and she seemed nervous as she talked with us. She told us that her father had gone up to Minto for supplies earlier that day and that she was alone there, in charge of keeping her father's record book of visitors. Looking at some of the names in the book, we found that Skip Burns's party had been in Fort Selkirk for the past two days and Lois said that we had missed them by only an hour. I asked Lois if I might take her picture, but she simply said "No" and hurried back into the cabin.

Rich and I looked at each other, shrugged, and then walked on down to the main buildings of Selkirk, where we spent the next two hours exploring the fascinating time machine that is Fort Selkirk. A little imagination can put goods of 70 years ago back into the remaining showcases in the two-story "Taylor and Drury Ltd., Estab. 1899" store: That same imagination can also renew the weathered dogsled that lies in a rambling barn next door, to send it forth into the freezing winter on some desperate mission. It is even an easy thing to populate the surrounding homes with sturdy citizens and set them to work over the pumps and wooden washing machines that still remain.

The greatest trip back into time came with a visit to the tiny one-room school house that stands slightly apart from the rest of the buildings, nearest the river. The walls still display ABC posters and aged maps that divide the world into long-vanished countries. The school desks are still in place, filled with children's writing materials, and a great iron stove dominates the center of the room, ready to do battle with the winter cold when the ice on the river outside is ten feet thick.

Rich and I finally completed our wanderings about the old buildings, marveling at all the human history they held, and began walking back up the line of buildings toward our boats. When we came to the Roberts' small cabin and its howling dogs, I felt compelled to try again for a photo of shy Lois Roberts. I walked toward the door of the cabin and had nearly reached it when Lois came outside, this time carrying a small husky puppy in her arms.

"My father doesn't like strangers to be near here," she said in her very soft voice, and again I thought she seemed nervous. "One of the dogs might break loose." This was not a contrived concern. The sled dogs in the north are tied up for the entire summer, and they become surly and mean waiting for the winter and action to return. I asked Lois again if I might take her picture and she reluctantly agreed, probably feeling that it was the only

Running water and washing machine.

way to get rid of this bothersome man from off the river. She seemed quite relieved when we said goodbye and walked away over the grassy field. Rich agreed that she undoubtedly was concerned at being so utterly alone, with two strange men, and later, in Dawson, we learned from Skip Burns that Lois's mother was most certainly also there in the cabin. I can't help but wonder if she wasn't—quite understandably—standing armed behind the door the whole time we talked with her daughter.

As we paddled down the Yukon from Selkirk, the headwind kicked up again, making forward progress difficult. As we passed Victoria Rock, a giant stone parapet which sheers down into the river and cuts off Selkirk's plain, Rich decided to relax and drift for the rest of the evening. I was in the mood for progress, however, so I picked out a point on the topo map—Selwyn, some 35 miles away around five curves of the river—and told Rich that I was going on and that I would probably see him in Dawson.

Beyond Victoria Rock, the river plunged into a land of high canyon walls that lined the river and made it seem dark even in the early evening, although they also helped cut the wind until it had died to nothing. That evening was very strange and beautiful, set as it was at the bottom of those long, twisting canyons of columnar basalt rock rising as high as 450 feet above the river. I was in deep shadow most of the time, but occasionally the high walls drew back slightly and allowed the sun to slant down to the river. The headwind ceased entirely, and the river became still and serene in the dusky light. I paddled energetically at first, but finally could not resist the tranquility of my surroundings and ended by sitting back with my elbows on the paddle, enjoying the sight of the black canyon walls and the many green river islands sliding by.

I had not gone very far into the canyon when I saw a swan swimming in the water ahead of me. I paddled down on it, amazed at the effortless speed it maintained ahead of me, but at last I got too close and it flapped and kicked ponderously up into the air. The huge bird flew downriver with heavy majesty, and when it got high enough, its great white body shone in the sun far above the dark river. Twenty minutes later I came upon the bird again, and again enjoyed watching the same ponderous ascent, the same regal sweeping of the air. The third time I caught up with it and sent it aloft, a spark of reason must have entered the small mind in that great white body, because once the swan climbed into the air, it wheeled around and flew back up the river.

Further downstream, when I was beginning to wonder if I really wanted to get to Selwyn that evening, I spotted a movement along the shore: A fat porcupine was waddling noisily through the dry poplar leaves along the bank. I paddled over, hoping for a photo despite the dim light, but the porky refused to pose. Instead, as soon as it became aware of my presence, it stuck its head into a depression in the muddy wall of the riverbank and flapped its bristling tail. Holding onto an overhanging branch, I stayed on, hoping the porcupine might leave its defensive position. Every now and then my prickly friend would pull its head back from the bank, look dimly around and spot me, then bury its head again and flap its tail to drive me off. I finally gave in and paddled away.

It was late and I was very tired when I finally reached Selwyn. I knew I was there only because I had been counting the curves in the canyon that the river has carved here. Selwyn proved to be a very uninviting place, however—a single tumbled-down, dank-looking cabin nearly swallowed by the dark brush around it—so I moved on to a brush-choked island a bit around the corner from Selwyn. I was just checking out the campsite possibilities when to my surprise Rich came into view, paddling like a maniac. He passed by before he could get to the island I was standing on, and since the island really wasn't very promising anyway, I hopped

Lois Roberts and friend.

back into the boat and followed after him. When I caught up, he told me that he'd drifted for an hour or so after I'd left him and then had become imbued with a sudden burst of energy and had been paddling ever since.

We continued for a mile or so and found a small grassy point backed by brush at the lower end of an island. We quickly set up camp, and over dinner Rich made me green with envy when he told how he had barreled directly down on a moose cow standing by the water's edge suckling a calf. He swore that he got perfect pictures as the current carried him silently by just a few feet from the scene, and I muttered threats of pirating his film at the earliest opportunity. I was dissatisfied throughout the trip with the small amount of wildlife I saw along the river's edge. Perhaps the scarcity was due to the unusually high water, or the lateness of the summer. Yet other people I met in the course of the trip had tales of having seen great hordes of animals. The group of six zanies at Big Salmon spoke at length, for example, about drifting practically into the paws of a startled grizzly standing erect on the shore of Thirty Mile. Arrrgggghh!

June 20, the fourteenth day on the river, the eleventh of actual travel, began with a somewhat sparse breakfast of crackers and jelly: I just didn't feel like fixing anything more. Rich and I set off from our little island point about 9:30, paddling out into a river flowing along smoothly under a bright blue sky. It was a lovely day, but for some reason the process of traveling seemed more of a duty than a joy to me. Rich seemed to be feeling about the same, and I suspect that the long days were beginning to tell on us: This was to be the fifth consecutive day that we had averaged more than 60 miles. In any case, while the day's travel down the river has faded into an indistinct haze, the events on shore that day stand out in sharp relief.

Our first stop, Coffee Creek, lies about 30 miles downriver from our island of the night before, and we reached it in a little over three hours. In reading through the brief descriptive notes on the river sites that Innes-Taylor had sent me, I had learned that "Coffee Creek has cabins and an old trading post remaining. A trail leads from the Yukon River into the back country and was a route used to the Chisana Gold Rush of 1913 in Alaska." How could one possibly pass by such an attraction?

We had kept track of our position all morning by counting the curves of the river through the high canyon walls that had begun at Selkirk. Coffee Creek, the map told us, would be reached after we had passed through six of these alternating curves. We had worked our way through all of them except the last and were halfway through that, looking not only for the settlement but for the actual stream after which the community is named. We were thirsty, and since the Yukon is so silty and not really too pleasant to drink, we were constantly looking for a gurgling brook cascading down some clean rock face directly into the river, or at least a stream that did not dump down into a scum-covered still-water cut before reaching the Yukon.

Reaching the Coffee Creek area, I plunged into what proved to be a complex network of little islands and still waterways, trying to find the creek the map said was there. I came out again quickly enough, unsuccessful in my search; but even in that brief time I could feel a sense of rising panic at being cut off and lost in an endless maze. I knew then how those Hollywood convicts felt wandering through the Florida Everglades. It was a distinct pleasure to return to the main river.

A few minutes later we pulled back to shore, having spotted the first remnants of the Coffee Creek settlement. The two or three cabins of this portion of Coffee Creek stood in a small clearing hemmed by the ever-present thick green underbrush, mostly alder and willow, that covers the river islands and lines the shore. After getting out of the Quisnam and stretching away the stiffness of three hours of paddling, I scrambled up the bank to the cabins and discovered that a startling blaze of wild roses carpeted the entire clearing in which the cabins stood. As I was looking about, marveling at the unexpected splash of color they produced, I became aware of the sound of bells. The sound pulled me away from the cabins and down a path, through several more clearings in the shrubbery, each resplendent with the small red and violet roses. At last I came to the source of the sound, three big work-horses with bells about their necks, tethered in one of the clearings. Beyond stood another set of cabins; and walking between them, I found myself being stared at in some disbelief by four men—two men and two boys, actually—sitting around a table by a cooktent at the edge of a field-like clearing.

I was indeed something to stare at, dressed as I was with my mosquito headnet, my camera dangling from my neck and gross rubber boots anchoring me heavily to the ground. My new-found acquaintances obviously weren't particularly concerned about the mosquito scourge in the neighborhood, since they were wearing short-sleeved shirts. They were also wearing cowboy boots and hats, and I felt very much the ridiculous city intruder.

Building in Coffee Creek.

"Come down the river, did you?" one of them grunted, the question almost a statement, as if that were the only possible thing such an apparition could possibly be doing. I admitted that that was so and learned from this first talkative fellow that they were homesteading. The other man, standing back in the cooktent now, interrupted with even shorter phrases to say that they were leasing, actually, since that avoided a homesteading land survey which might cost up to $3,000. It all seemed rather confused, even among them, because when I asked what they were going to do with the land, they all looked a little blank until one of them mumbled "hay farming," and then *I* looked a little blank when another allowed as how they didn't plan to sell any hay anyway.

Then occurred one of those silly things that you kick yourself for for days after they happen. I was standing, looking out across the field, wondering how I might either say something intelligent or disappear from under the silent scrutiny of these four, when I realized that the man standing in the cooktent had said something to me. He was obviously the one in charge and seemed the toughest of the lot (I thought I could see the mosquitoes denting their probosci against his skin). "Beg pardon?" I said, and he repeated his question: "Take cream or sugar in your tea?" And I'll be damned

The intrepid kayaker, below Coffee Creek.

if I didn't react with some sort of inbred caution we've developed to cope with our complex urban life. "Oh, no, no thanks, thank you very much. I better be getting along."

I am still embarassed about it. Here was this gruff homesteader offering tea and friendship to some fool Cheechako come stumbling in from the river, and I refused his offer! How absolutely stupid, how absurd! It was these very people that I wanted to make contact with along the river, and I had shied away even as they invited me to join them.

My mind was churning with recriminations as I walked back along the paths through the clearings to the first cabins and the boats. Rich seemed to have slumped into the same sort of tired frame of mind as I had and showed little interest in the strangers I had met. He *was* interested, however, when I told him that the four men had seen Skip's tour go past in the late afternoon the day before. We seemed to be doing rather well in our chase to catch up with Skip, considering that we were matching paddles and oars against Skip's 40-horsepower outboards.

The next few hours on the river passed by uneventfully. At one point I gave Rich my camera and asked him to take a few photos of me churning up and down the river, but I soon gave up that endeavor when the upstream paddling made me dizzy. Moving against the current often had that effect, with the banks sliding backward past you despite your energetic paddling. It is much like looking at the world from between your legs or trying to run along a beach as the foam under your feet slides back to the ocean.

We continued downriver until evening, when Rich and I decided to try something different: We would stop for dinner, then push on for a few hours before camping for the night. Thus, a little over 15 miles from Coffee Creek, we pulled the boats up on a narrow strip of rather steeply slanting shoreline and set about fixing a meal. As was too often the case, my stove seemed to be on strike that evening, so I borrowed Rich's magnificently effective and practical Optimus and cooked up an excellent meal of macaroni and cheese.

As we were eating I happened to look across the river to an island and noticed several logs piled on its upper end. One of the logs was a shade or two lighter than the rest in the evening sun. I looked at it for quite a long time, wondering if it just might be alive. It almost looked like a horse, or a moose, but it was so still. Finally I asked Rich's opinion, and he glanced up, assured me the object was inanimate, and went back to his meal. A few minutes later he nudged me and said "Sorry about that," indicating the spot, now empty, where my light-colored log had been. The perfect moose photo, missed!

As I loudly lamented this missed opportunity, we became aware of the sound of a motorboat coming down the river toward us. The sound was echoing off the hills and islands all around, but it took a long time for the boat to actually pass by. (The echoes on the river are extraordinary; quite often, when I was alone on the river, I would whistle and sing in two and even three-part harmony.) We waved as the boat, a smaller model of the long, flat-nosed riverboats we'd seen at Little Salmon and Minto, finally putt-putted by carrying an intriguing group. The four occupants, two men and two women, were all bundled up, one couple sitting far forward of a large pile of equipment hidden under a tarp, the other back in the rear of the boat. They all looked quite old and rather urban for a Yukon excursion, but they also looked very vigorous and happy as they waved. The way the boat was handled also suggested that at least one of them was at home in this region of the world.

Rich and I finished dinner and got back into our boats, only to get back out again just a few minutes later at the buildings of Kirkman Creek. The site is privately owned now, although the mining settlement originally included a functioning post office. We climbed up to the meadow that surrounds the cabins that remain and discovered that the old folks who had passed us were coming up from another direction. We smiled broadly, since we were trespassing, and I asked if they happened to be the owners. The woman who led the procession—heavy and essential, an earthmother of a woman—said "No" but that they knew the owners. They had been intending to stay further down the river, in another set of cabins but had found them so filled with trash and in such disarray that they had returned to the meadows of Kirkman Creek to set up their tents. As we talked with the woman the three others were busy setting up two very large upright canvas tents, the distant and heavy ancestors to our lightweight nylon ones. The woman, whose name was Martha, explained slyly that she was "the Queen Bee of this crowd" and that her companions were her loyal workers. Then she exclaimed over how nice the evening was, while a whole clan of mosquitoes dined unnoticed on her bare arms.

Martha and her husband, Cam Cameron, were the guides for this trip, taking their friends the Murphys of Seattle down the Yukon from Whitehorse to Dawson for what Martha called "a final look at the old river." Both Martha Cameron and Dave Murphy were born in Dawson while the gold rush was still recent history, but he had not been back there for years. The Camerons were well-suited to act as guides on the river, since Cam had served as a Mounty in the area for years—most recently from 1935 to 1949 at Fort Selkirk, when that town still had a population of 15 whites and 90 Indians. He looked very much the way a retired Mounty should look: tall, white haired and mustached, slightly stooped but still strong, a gentle expression on his face, with blue eyes that held the necessary distant look about them. We helped the Camerons and Murphys unload their boat, and then I took a photo of the four. With the tents up, their lawn chairs set out between, wild roses all about, the two couples looked as though they had lived comfortably in that clearing all their lives.

We talked for a while longer, then said goodbye to these delightful people and walked back to the boats. Goaded by Rich's boasts about the moose cow and calf he had seen the night before, I decided to go moose hunting before stopping to camp that evening. So Rich slid on down the river while I cut across to the islands that were still bathed in the bright evening sunlight. Almost immediately I found success. I was moving along a perfectly flat small island, covered with brush and barely above the water, when I suddenly realized I had passed two moose grazing in the shrubbery. I turned the boat and worked back against the current into a still backwater, then drifted silently up almost to the feet of the huge creatures. Finally they spotted me, stared for a moment, still chewing, then snorted and charged away through the plants they had been devouring.

I took several photos coming up on them; then, after they charged away, I paddled around the island and found them again for another photo or two. They never really emerged from the cover, and I had forgotten to put a long enough lens on my camera beforehand, so my photos offered little more than proof that something big and vaguely moose-like was indeed lurking in the bushes of the Yukon. Yet I was pleased with the success of my mini-safari, for I had correctly guessed that moose might be found browsing on the low islands of the river in the late evening, and I had gained an excellent close-up impression of the size and shape of these shy beasts. With this success it seemed a beautiful evening, and I flew down the smooth and now dark river for the next hour, paddling strenuously to catch up with Rich.

Cam and Martha Cameron, seated; Dave and Margaret Murphy, standing.

11   A Short Chapter: Stewart Island and on to Dawson

I was just waking when Rich went by my tent the next morning, muttered that he would see me at Stewart Island 15 miles down the river, climbed into his boat and took off. The night before we had made the same mistake we always made, that of starting to look for a campsite when we were tired and ready to stop. It took us miles to find a suitable place, and that spot required that we make another of our frantic races against the current across most of the width of the river. Rich most certainly had not been in a good mood as the previous day drew to a close, and he still seemed to be carrying a little charge of irritation at things in general. He was in no state of mind to put up with waiting for me to get ready to depart this morning. So I said "Sure, see you," and snuggled back into my sleeping bag for a bit more rest. I was camped just above my boat, on a small bed of soft fern-like green plants under the ever-present willow and alder shrubbery of the islands, and the sun couldn't reach me to disturb my comfort.

The evening before, while setting up my tent, I had found the complete skull and antlers of a huge moose, which weighed at least 60 pounds. I went to sleep wondering how I might mount them on the front of my kayak, to render real class and a certain *savoir faire* to the Quisnam. Now, when I finally emerged from the tent, I spent the next hour photographing the head and myself from all different angles, having decided that this was the only practical way to at least partially preserve my find. The mosquitoes were buzzing around most hungrily, so in addition to the headnet I was forced to don my rain parka and gloves to ward them off. In the photos I look like a Martian again, puzzling over some fossilized monster's skull.

Although I certainly couldn't carry the antlers with me, I also couldn't bear to leave my find hidden in the bushes, unadmired by anyone else. So I hauled them out to the river bank and I set them up facing the river. I was sure the antlers would be seen by anyone passing by because the bank here looked as though it had been plowed between brush and water, swept clean to the bare earth by the action of the river ice churning along during break-up. I wrote my name and address in small letters on one

My great moose skull find, part of which found its way to Berkeley.

of the antlers, adding a note asking that whoever found the antlers might write to me and let me know who they were and where they were from. (Two months later I found the piece of horn carrying my note in my mailbox in Berkeley. The antlers had been found by a couple who live in San Francisco!)

With the antlers propped up and inscribed, I bundled my things and myself into the kayak and dashed out onto the river to escape the relentless mosquitoes. Almost immediately I managed to run aground; I had tried to cut to the right of a low bar and had ignored the tell-tale ripples that indicated shallow water. Running aground, even briefly, is a scary affair. At the same time that the kayak anchors itself on the rocks below, the river current continues to push at it, turning it broadside and threatening to roll it over. And as you struggle to remain upright, you are tormented by the terrible grinding sounds coming from the rocks against that thin rubber hull. I was aground for only a moment, but the experience did encourage me to avoid doing it again in the future.

A few minutes after freeing myself from the few shallow rocks I had encountered, I passed the point on the left beyond which the White River enters the Yukon, carrying great quantities of silt from the glaciers of the St. Elias mountain range far to the south. I paddled about looking for the line the two rivers are said to make when joining, but finally decided that the Yukon was so silty itself that the line must be nearly invisible at that time of year. A little further on, I heard the noise of a motorboat echoing down the river, and a few minutes later the Camerons and Murphys went chugging by me again, waving and smiling.

The channel above Stewart Island is rather full of islands, the most that I had seen so far on the river, and I began to worry that I might miss Stewart Island, and its store, in such a maze. I needn't have worried. The Burien's store on Stewart Island has a red roof that couldn't possibly be missed: I guess that when all of your commerce comes from people traveling down a wide river, you make sure that they can see your place of business. I guided the kayak on what I thought was a tight course along the right shore, but I still had to paddle hard to keep from being swept past the docking area that held Rich's canoe, the Cameron's boat and one or two other boats. I got to the vertical dirt bank of the island, stepped out precariously, tied the boat to something that looked stable, then climbed up the crumbling dirt wall almost into the arms of Rudy Burien, the proprietor of the store—and the island.

Rudy Burien is a little leather-skinned elf of a man, with bright eyes of uncommon sharpness; he saw me coming down the river a good ten minutes before Rich spotted me. Rudy and his family have managed the island's store since 1951; and before that, he and his wife had run a roadhouse on the island during the last years of the steamer trade on the river. Their little enclave consisted of several sheds, his store, a substantial home, several cabins for rent to travelers and, further back from the water, a building housing a wealth of historic goods they have gleaned from ruins all up and down the river. Scattered among these human dwellings are smaller habitations for the Burien's colony of sled dogs, all of them chained and noisy but friendly and eager for attention.

Living on Stewart Island must be an exciting affair, if for no other reason than wondering each morning if your land is still there. The river takes up to 30 feet of the island each year, and the store and several of the other buildings have twice been moved back from the advancing water with the aid of a cat Rudy keeps handy for the purpose. Originally, Stewart Island was a complete little community, with a post office, telegraph station, some trapper's cabins and a trading post. All of these structures are now gone, claimed by the passing water.

The welcoming committee at Stewart Island.

Burien's store on Stewart Island.

After talking with Mr. Burien for a while, I wandered into the Burien store for a nutritious breakfast of canned apple juice, canned raspberries and a box of some vile sort of cookies. As I ate I looked over the other goods the store had to offer, including a number of wolf-pelts and a magnificent wolf-fur parka, beautiful to look at and incredibly soft to the touch. The furs were also incredibly expensive (the pelts were $150 each), and it was just as well that I was torn away from my shopping by bright-cheeked and energetic Mrs. Burien, who invited me to join Rich, the Camerons and Murphys and the rest of her family inside her kitchen for a second breakfast of tea and delicious hot rolls and butter. It was a very enjoyable way to spend the rest of the morning, luxuriating in the creature comforts of that warm kitchen and talking with these very pleasant people.

At one point Rudy happened to be explaining why he didn't have any farm animals about his place, and in a remark he tossed off I think he summed up his life philosophy: "Animals mean fences," he said, "and I don't like fences." In the summer he and his wife and youngest son Ivan sell goods to whomever drops by from the river, while an older son does some mining back in the hills. In the winter the men engage in a little trapping. Although the family appears to be very removed from civilization,

Fauna and flora, Olgilvie.

living alone as they do out in an empty wilderness, they are actually only a day away from Dawson and have 300 neighbors within a reasonable distance. The life the Buriens have created is very appealing, and I wish we could have spent more time with them. But before too many hours had passed, the travel ethic grabbed us again, and Rich and I found ourselves shaking hands with our hosts and saying goodbye.

The river's current seemed to have grown sluggish beyond Stewart Island, and we had to work hard to cover the 25 miles to the site of Ogilvie, hidden on the right bank of the river behind a large island. Ogilvie was named after William Ogilvie, the incorruptible government surveyor who mapped out Dawson and most of the gold fields of the Klondike and was later Commissioner of the Yukon Territory. The town of Ogilvie was the location of the oldest post office in the Yukon Territory, but today it consists only of three ruined log cabins falling back into the ground in a rapidly disappearing clearing in the brush.

Rich did not feel like continuing much beyond Ogilvie, whereas Dawson was becoming such a very strong goal for me that I wanted to get as close to it as possible that evening. So I told Rich that I would see him in Dawson the next day and paddled off into

The Olgilvie post office, the oldest in Yukon Territory.

the lengthening evening shadows. The sky began to cloud over as I traveled, and it was drizzling slightly when, several hours later, I finally found a small island meadow in which to make camp for the night. I camped with my tent set in the angle of two low dirt walls, all that remained of someone's residence by the river.

That evening brought the final break in relations between me and my Swedish stove, which shall be nameless. I was forced inside the tent by the occasional rain and constant mosquitoes, and I had lovely visions of enjoying a warm meal while lying comfortably within the tent, laughing smugly at the pests and rain outside. Very carefully, very calmly, I set about getting that stove to light. I struggled with it for 45 minutes, going through the whole ridiculous series of steps needed to light the thing: First, I carefully warmed it with my hands to get the gas flowing properly—with no result. Then I tried a scrap of burning paper to warm it—zero. Finally, I built a bonfire that threatened to burn down the tent —again, nothing. I ended by quietly consigning that wretched stove to the deepest regions of hell, then calmly, very calmly, threw the damn thing into a corner and ate crackers and cheese for supper.

12   Dawson, City of Gold

The city of Dawson burst into existence as a tent town on both sides of the mouth of the Klondike in the spring of 1897. Its population was made up by those few men fortunate enough to be in the region the year before when word of George Carmack's discovery of gold on Rabbit Creek spread like a wildfire along the river. At the time, this makeshift city beside the Yukon undoubtedly held the greatest percentage of potential millionaires—millionaires whose wealth for the most part still lay waiting beneath the frozen ground—of any city in history. Ironically, many of these men of future wealth suffered the torments of scurvy, since all the gold in the world couldn't buy fresh vegetables in Dawson that winter.

A year later, under the impact of the world's last great gold stampede, Dawson's population fluctuated between 15,000 and 25,000 people. The gold drew men and goods and a few women, most of whom planned to mine the miners, from all over the planet to this cramped site at the mouth of the Klondike. Building lots on the swampy wedge of land between the Klondike and the Yukon Rivers sold for up to $40,000 each, and luxuries seen only in the greatest cities of the outside world became available where, only a year before, even the necessities were cruelly scarce. Dawson boiled with vitality, instantly rebuilding what was destroyed when three major fires and numerous smaller blazes roared through its jerry-built wooden buildings, so that the process of parting the miners from their gold might continue unimpeded.

The men who were drawn to the Yukon endured all the hardships of their journey in the belief that "gold for the taking" awaited them in the Klondike. This idea was encouraged by companies and organizations throughout the world that stood to gain from such a mass migration: transportation firms, equipment and food suppliers, and even the cities through which these men had to travel. *Caveat emptor*—buyer beware—was the rule and law of this age, and unscrupulous men all over the world dangled the specter of unlimited gold before the eyes of hungry men, to part them from what coins their pockets already held. Many of the men in the United States who responded to the call were literally hungry, since at the time of the strike the country was in the grip of one of its most severe depressions. The gold which they were going to gather so easily made those men who persevered in their frenzied dream strong enough to carry the NWMP-required ton of supplies over the torturous, icy Chilkoot Pass in the dead of winter and down to the frozen lakes at the head of the Yukon. There they cut trees and whipsawed them one by one into planks for the leaking boats they threw together for the last leg of their race to Dawson.

The men of the "Rush of '98" suffered unbelievable hardship and punishment to reach their goal, and most of them spent far more money in the process than they were ever to take out of the goldfields. For by the time they reached the Klondike, all the creek beds for miles around George Carmack's discovery on Rabbit'Creek, renamed Bonanza Creek, were staked by those men already on the scene the year before. The rumors that brought these valiant but naive new seekers after gold were hopelessly out of date even before they were launched by the arrival of Dawson's first millionaires with their sacks of gold in the cities of the West Coast the previous summer. Most of the men of '98 left Dawson almost as soon as they arrived, carrying with them only the memories of the punishment they had undergone. By the summer of 1899 it was all over. Most of Dawson's remaining population was drawn away down the river by news of a new gold strike in Nome, Alaska, and the town was left to wane to today's population of roughly 300 permanent inhabitants.

The gold seekers who poured down the Yukon in 1898 were told that they would know Dawson by the great slash of bare rock that cut into the face of a hill called Midnight Dome. A little after 11 a.m. on June 22, I paddled around a bend in the river and saw the unmistakable signpost ahead. I stopped paddling and simply rode along with the river, looking about and feeling that tingle of success and relief which accompanies the attainment of any special goal.

By reaching the town of Dawson, I had traveled through almost 500 miles of Canadian wilderness by kayak, I had encountered at first hand the country which had stirred millions to thoughts of gold and incited more than 100,000 to set out after it, and I had experienced the historic river in the classic way, aboard a tiny craft powered by my own efforts. I had been drawn down the river by thoughts of reward, like the early gold stampeders, although my image of that reward was couched in such terms as "experience," "adventure," and even "self-knowledge." Dawson

The slash on Midnight Dome, with Dawson below it.

had been the goal that had taken me down this first portion of the Yukon, and now it stood just ahead, waiting for my arrival.

I was quite surprised at how different the Dawson country was from my mental expectations. Undoubtedly influenced by the Sierra Nevada, I had set the Klondike and its tributaries into high granite country, covered with pines and clear streams falling from pool to deep green pool down the mountainsides. In fact, the country around Dawson is rolling hill country, strikingly similar to the foothills of California behind Sacramento. And, of course, that isn't so very strange, since both areas are the kind of placer country in which gold is found. The only real difference lay in the vegetation which covered these hills: thick stands of poplar, black spruce, alder and willow, in contrast to the oak and pines of the California gold country.

As I floated toward the mouth of the Klondike, with the buildings of Dawson beyond, I looked hard at a small flat that I was passing, but I could see no signs of its somewhat lurid past: The flat was once known as Lousetown, where Dawson's girls of easy virtue were domiciled and sharp-eyed Dawson wives could watch through the bright summer nights to make sure that their men didn't cross the bridge between the communities for comfort in someone else's arms.

I beached the kayak at the foot of the steep bank atop which runs Dawson's Front Street. The bank also serves as a dike between the city and its river, offering some protection against the flooding which used to be common during spring break-up. I climbed up the bank, stood for a long minute looking down the dusty street to the town center on my left and out over the nearly empty city before me, then turned and walked south back up the river to the RCMP office. Inside, a pleasant young officer in the distinctive RCMP uniform—spurs and all—looked up, grinned, and said "Well, you're just off the river, aren't you!" It was pretty obvious. I was wearing my rumpled grey sweatshirt, dirty jeans, rubber boots, a slouch hat, three weeks of beard, and my melodramatic hunting knife. The officer pulled out the information sheet that told of my presence on the river and marked me as having arrived in the alloted time; then he warned me against leaving my kayak on the city side of the river, repeating what so many people had said about things having a way of walking off. He suggested that I camp at a public campground directly across the river and use the ferry, which, as an integral part of the highway through Dawson to Alaska, operates for all but one hour throughout the week. The officer then added, perhaps with a slight sense of the self-interest of his town, that showers were available for people traveling through the town at a motel on Fifth Avenue.

I thanked him, went back to the boat, and pulled out into the river once again to cross over to his suggested campground. As I paddled hurriedly across I could see that two of Skip Burns's floatboats were drawn up on a flat below the Bank of Commerce on Front Street, and the third was waiting for me on the small beach below the campground. A moment after I beached my own craft, Skip's unmistakable thatch of red hair appeared over the hill, and I found myself enveloped in a greeting worthy of long-lost friends. Skip was astonished at the speed Rich and I had made down the river, and he was equally astonished to learn that the coil of excellent rope that had mysteriously appeared in his equipment belonged to Rich.

Skip, one of his charges and I hopped into his floatboat, and we churned back across the river. Skip was busy arranging to take some German film makers on a river tour of the Dawson area, so I said that I would see him later and walked back up to Front Street again. I was torn between three pressing needs: a shower, food, and getting mail at the post office. I finally gave the post office first priority and found my choice rewarded with

*The free ferry, Dawson, an integral link in the
Whitehorse, Dawson, Alaska Highway.*

several letters from friends in the outside world. These were read
as I solved my next most important need with a lunch of bacon
and eggs in a diner built into a mobile home back on Front Street.
After lunch I crossed back over the river to set up my tent and
write several letters in response to the ones I'd received. And
then it was time to ferry back to town for that ultimate delight,
a shower. The Northwestern Motel, some five blocks back from
the river, had showers and a laundromat in a small side building.
They charged a dollar apiece, and I would have happily paid twice
the price for the joy of sluicing off my ten day's accumulated grime.

Reeling from the pleasure of the shower and clean clothing,
I staggered from the motel down the road and into St. Paul's
Church, where three movies on Dawson and its surroundings were
being shown in return for donations to the church. There, I enjoyed
seeing for a second time one of the greatest documentary films
I have ever seen, Pierre Berton's "City of Gold." This film is
a lyrical portrayal of Dawson City as it was during its heyday,
beautifully counterpointed with scenes of how it was when the
film was made in the mid-fifties. Berton sends his viewers into
the depths of the monumental Hegg photographs of the gold seekers

struggling on Chilkoot and reveling in Dawson. Then he draws us back to the town of ruins and ruined men which was his native city in the fifties. Dawson today looks fresher and more alive than in Berton's film, but nothing else I have ever seen succeeds so well in carrying the former vigor and might of this City of Gold.

During the next day and a half, I drank as deeply of Dawson's reality and history as I possibly could. I absorbed the feel of its dirt streets, its abandoned, boarded-up buildings, its proud and hardy permanent citizenry, and its empty, barren gold-fields. The town of Dawson is a living museum, and I mightily enjoyed meandering through its artifacts.

My evenings—and Rich's, since he had joined me a few hours after my arrival—were devoted to performances of the Dawson Gaslight Follies. These are held in the Palace Grand Theater, which was restored to its original splendor in 1961–62 by the Canadian Department of Northern Affairs. The Palace Grand was built in 1899 by Arizona Charlie Meadows to resemble a miniature European opera house, although I doubt any European opera house allowed the goings-on in its box seats that were regular practice in the boxes here in Dawson: History mentions something about rich miners shutting the curtains on their boxes for rather more private entertainments while the public show went on below.

Today the Palace Grand is again the scene for shows, put on by a cast of young actors and actresses drawn from all over Canada for the summer season. Anyone walking by the theater before showtime is encouraged to "Come on in, folks" by "Klondike Sue" Ward–Speare, a gregarious woman who has enjoyed barking for Dawson's theater for the last several years. She hustles up an audience—easily done as this is one of Dawson's prime attractions —then rushes inside and talks up the show and the other attractions in Dawson. One of her instructions to the audience is that they must involve themselves in the show, participating with any sort of remarks they think appropriate. As a result, throughout the skits of the Follies, some rather rude suggestions came floating toward the stage, and the actors dropped their lines to deal with the better ones in truly masterful and amusing ways. The alternating show at the Palace Grand was "The Drunkard," a straight melodrama, which seemed to give the audience equal pleasure.

Another high point of my stay in Dawson was the "Gold City Tour: See and Hear History of Dawson and the Goldfield. An Interesting Three Hour Tour"—all of which left from the Northwestern Motel of the Great Shower Experience. Normally, I detest tours, because too frequently one is paying inordinate amounts for the right to be a sardine among many other sardines, with the likelihood of seeing little or nothing of the object of interest. But at the time I could think of no other way to get out to the goldfields easily. As it turned out, I am very glad that I was forced into taking this particular tour. It was splendid.

The tour left the motel at nine on a bright, warm and sunny morning, with seven of us crammed into a Mircobus. ("Right," I thought, "another sardine operation.") The driver and guide was Tim Cole, a marvelous man of about 60, with a string tie, white hair behind a receding hairline, glasses, and a gentle but enthusiastic voice. He was the reason for the excellence of the tour.

Tim Cole came to Dawson years ago and had actually mined along Bonanza Creek during his first years in the area. Thus, what he told us about Dawson and the goldfields was not out of history books but directly from his own memory and experience. As we drove up and down the streets of Dawson, looking at the old boarded-up buildings that listed to one side or another due to the melting permafrost beneath them, he told many personal anecdotes about the people he had known during his life in Dawson, and he succeeded in bringing the City of Gold back to life. For instance, the first house he had owned when he came to Dawson had previously been a bordello, a bit of historical background he learned only after several incidents in which men barged into his house unannounced. To keep that former establishment's still concupiscent clients away, Tim had to put up a huge sign, lit throughout the night, informing visitors that a family with children now occupied the premises. Tim added the "children" to give the sign more impact.

The stories went on and on as we drove about. At one point the bus passed a very neat little home far up on the hill behind Dawson, with bright flowers spilling out of planter boxes on the front porch. Tim explained that this was the residence of an 84-year-old man who had come into town from a year-round cabin on the creeks only because he felt his 83-year-old wife might someday need the services of the local hospital. The tour stopped at the cabin of poet Robert Service, and at Jack London's rough log shack. The latter was brought in from the Stewart River, where London had been trapped by the winter ice in 1897–1898. Half the original logs of the cabin are in the reconstruction in Dawson, while the other half went to a similar structure in Jack London Square in Oakland, California. The Service and London buildings are the most famous in Dawson, but much of the city seems like a historic graveyard, with the multitudes of empty buildings stand-

The Bonanza Creek home and garden of 84 year old miner, Pete Pamachema.

ing like faded and falling grave markers. But there is also a sense of rebirth about Dawson. With more and more tourists visiting the city, the local economy is beginning to revive, and Cole pointed out the several efforts of the local Historical Society to rebuild and renew many of the old decaying monuments to the past.

From the city, Tim drove out along the Klondike River, then turned right and followed the bucking dirt road along Bonanza Creek, where gold was found in such abundance. The country between the canyon ridges flanking the creek looks as if years of war had engulfed the area: It is bare of all but the briefest scrub, and huge rows of naked rock and rubble—tailings from the dredges—course back and forth along the creek like the leavings of some giant insect grub.

The earth on Bonanza has been sifted five times now, first by the original miners, then by larger mining companies, then by small dredges, next larger dredges, and finally by a giant dredge, one of the largest ever built, that was designed to suck the last bits of gold from the earlier tailings. To give some idea of the importance and power of gold, it is only necessary to quote some of the statistics on this final huge machine. The dredge was a floating barge measuring 140 feet from stem to stern, 65 feet wide.

Jack London's cabin in Dawson.

Its dredge-line consisted of 75 two-ton, 16-cubic-foot-capacity buckets, which gave the dredge a theoretical capacity of 18,000 cubic yards of gold-bearing gravel each day. One of the films in St. Paul's the evening before had shown the dredge in operation, and it seemed laughable that such an immense hulk of machinery should work so hard to produce mere handfuls of golden residue each day, like a whale laboring to produce a pea pod.

This dredge, along with the other 29 dredges of various sizes built at one time or another on the creeks of the Klondike, is silent now, stilled in 1959 when its operation no longer proved profitable. Now two of its five stories lie buried in the silt-filled pool in which it used to float, and the creeks have once again become the domain of moose and bear and the occasional single miner struggling to uncover those last few dollars worth of gold that may still lie hidden in the mutilated earth.

As we drove along Bonanza, Tim would often interrupt his spiel with stories about his own mining operations on the creek, which included such minor little pastimes as building eight miles of wooden flumes along the twisting hillsides in order to bring water to his mine. He also had many critical things to say about the current mining operations going on on the river. He would look out the window and notice some new effort, mutter that they wouldn't find anything *there*, that that spot had already been tried years ago. At another point he directed our attention to a man working over a pump engine beside a small dammed-up pool: "He'd better get that thing going," he said, "His dam's going to give way before tonight if he doesn't." He clearly knew what he was talking about; he had been through it all before.

The last stop of the tour was at a large streamside rock holding a plaque that commemorates the site where the Klondike gold rush began, where George Washington Carmack—"Siwash George the squawman"—discovered gold on Rabbit Creek. Actually, it was George's Indian brother-in-law Skookum Jim who was dazzled by the sight of gold when he stooped over the creek for a drink of water, but the Discovery Claim was filed in Carmack's name, and he took charge of telling the outside world. He recorded the date of his discovery—August 17th, 1896—in a blaze on a nearby spruce tree, then he and his Indian relatives set off down the Klondike and Yukon to Forty Mile, the closest population center, to alert the miners there of their find. Ironically, although Carmack told the world, he made no effort to tell Jim Henderson, the man who had suggested that he try the prospects on Rabbit Creek. Henderson, only a half-day's walk away, came out from his own lonely search for gold months later, to discover all of his small creek staked, and even its name changed from Rabbit to Bonanza. Thus, Henderson never got a dime's worth of dust out of the discovery he was at least in part responsible for. It's said that he made too clear to Carmack his aversion toward Indians, an aversion which cost him a fortune in the gold he had spent his life searching for.

As you stand in the small circle of roadway around the memorial stone to Carmack and his Discovery Claim, you look at the silent hills, the rubble of gravel underfoot, the small stands of willow trying to extend their lines through the barren river bottom, and find it hard to imagine the attraction that this small spot of earth radiated throughout the world. But with a little reading, and perhaps a look at the great Hegg photographs, it can be done. The story I love best concerns a Swede, Charley Anderson. Two men, Alfred Thayer and Winfield Oler, rushed up from Forty Mile and staked claim number 29 on the Bonanza, then returned the nearly 60 miles downriver to Forty Mile, doubtful that anything of value lay under their property. With the help of a great deal of alcohol, they talked Anderson, just back from a summer's work in the Sixty Mile River region, into handing over $800 he had gleaned from his labors in return for their claim. The next day a sober and broke Anderson tried to get Inspector Constantine of the NWMP to force the men to return his money, but the inspector regretfully informed him that there was nothing to be done. Anderson could only go out to his new possession and begin the laborious process of burning through the permafrost and scraping out the resulting mud, working his way down to bedrock to see if he had anything of value. Before he was done, Anderson's 500 feet of claim along the little creek paid him over a million dollars, and I wonder how Thayer and Oler felt about that.

The excitement throughout all this area must have been electric, as the miners realized what they had found. There were some 40 claims on the lower portion of the Eldorado, a small pup creek that ran into Bonanza above Discovery Claim. Each of these claims were 500 feet long, and the average value of gold in each *foot* of those claims was over $1,000. Think of the excitement of such a couple as Clarence and Ethyl Berry, a former farmer and waitress, who staked claim number 6 on Eldorado Creek. They were working the richest placer creek ever seen in all the world, from which they recorded single pan yields—two spadefuls of bedrock gravel—of over $500. To understand this, it helps to know that before the Klondike strike, eight *cents* a pan was considered good enough to merit further work.

Most of the men who suddenly had fortune thrust upon them in the Klondike lived to see it disappear almost as quickly as it had come. Charley Anderson, for example, died in a sawmill in Sapperton, British Columbia, working each month for a sum of money he would have found several times over in a pan of the Bonanza bedrock. He was broke even before the First World War, with only the memory of a wild and extravagent tour through Europe to show for it. All but a very few of the Klondike millionaires followed the same course, with only a difference in detail. The money these men had searched for through years of toil ran through their fingers like water, and many of them spent their last year hoping to repeat the incredible luck that fortune had once granted them.

The last thing I did in Dawson, excepting the downing of a final strawberry milkshake for strength, was to take the tour through the S.S. Keno, a paddlewheeler that stands high above the river on Front Street. It was raining lightly and this seemed like an excellent way to get under shelter. To my surprise and pleasure, I was the entire tour group, and my guide was a lovely freckle-faced and auburn-haired young lady named Ann Hutchins. The Keno

Sunset, taken from Dawson looking nearly due north at about midnight.

is not a particularly old ship, nor a very big one, but it is in good repair, and the Dawson City Tourist Association assigns some of its young women members, in period costume, to tell tourists about the size of the paddles and the reason for the boilers and such. I'm afraid I didn't hear very much of Ann's spiel about pressure in the engine room or the number of passengers who used to cram the upper deck, but I certainly admired her as she dutifully led me all about the ship. Up on the top deck, standing high above the rooftops of Dawson, we ended the tour and began to talk about Ann. I learned that she and her husband (rats!) were homesteading a farm just up from Dawson on the river. She told me how they had spent the previous year living in Dawson, in a small cabin far up on the hill behind the city, and about the animals which would come to nose about during the long light hours of the summer. She also talked about their hopes for their farm, and their future, and it all sounded wonderful. Dawson is coming alive again, and these are the sort of young people who are restoring it.

After this talk with Ann, I realized that I was ready to leave Dawson. I had enjoyed myself enormously over the past two days. But there is something about discovering other people's happiness that often causes you to want to move on, since all too often you realize that you cannot join in, at least at the moment. Dawson was a fascinating place, and I think that anyone, given the right circumstances, could carve out a very admirable life there. But at this point my life involved the river flowing past Dawson rather than the city itself, and I felt that it was time to get back onto the river. I thanked Ann, found Rich, who was also ready to leave, and we crossed the river on the ferry for the last time. I dismantled my camp, packed away $20 worth of new food supplies, and set off after Rich, who as always was loaded and away before me.

We moved down the Yukon into the teeth of a whipping head-wind, under a boring grey sky from which rain misted down. The ferry pilot tooted as I went stroking by, and I waved my thanks to him for his services back and forth across the river. Dawson had been an excellent goal to strive for, an excellent place to stop; but it was good to be sliding away from the town and its people, moving down the river and into my own private world of at least nominal self-reliance and tranquility.

13   Onward: Forty Mile and Eagle, Alaska

The river stretches straight north from Dawson for two or three miles, passing by the abandoned Indian village of Moosehide, which now figures as a tourist attraction in the Dawson scheme of things. Beyond, the river bends to the left out of sight of the city, plunging the traveler back into remote and wild surroundings. Eight miles below Dawson I stopped at the site of Fort Reliance. The fort, now only a pile of logs and a deep depression on a bluff high above the river, was built by Leroy Napoleon "Jack" McQuesten in 1874 and was abandoned in 1886 after serving, off and on, as a trading post and center for the gradually increasing prospecting activity that went on in the region. Ironically, McQuesten, intensely concerned with the search for gold, thought of the streams and hills just a few short miles above his fort as good only for moose pasture, and he never reaped the huge rewards that might have been his.

After Fort Reliance, it began to rain in earnest and continued to pour down for the next 15 miles. The river's surface was choppy, its mud-colored contents whipped by a heavy headwind that made travel painful, not only slowing progress but driving the rain into my face and down my neck. Both Rich and I were hunched over against the elements, straining to keep control of the boats and to find a satisfactory stroking rhythm in the damp and chill. The view down the river was bleak, showing either rain-drenched vistas in the distance or walls of cold fog close at hand. Rich and I paddled along together for a while, but then we separated, probably because we both felt that we didn't need the sight of the other's cold discomfort added to our own. When I finally spotted a sandbar above water at the head of an island, I was more than willing to stop, despite having made only a little over 20 miles in four hours of intermittent paddling.

I made for the island, only to find myself aground a dozen yards from shore. Things were frantic for a moment or two as the kayak swirled and rolled sideways on its point of contact, but I solved the problem by simply leaping out of the Quisnam and towing it to the beach. Of course, I got wet almost to my waist, but at this point that didn't matter a great deal. Rich, taking an obvious and easier route to the beach, paddled by just as I was striding along through the river. He wondered aloud about the curious time and place I had chosen for taking a stroll, and I thanked him very politely for his concern and attention.

I stomped ashore and hurriedly went about setting up my tent and unloading the boat. I was very wet and cold by now, and most anxious to get out of the wind, into some dry clothes and in front of some hot food. Of course, the latter hope was dependent on the infernal stove, but perhaps it caught some sense of my temper: It consumed only a half hour of my time before it grudgingly heated some spanish rice to a tolerable warmth. The whole while I was struggling over that confounded mechanical monstrosity, I could hear Rich's stove happily roaring away. When I had finished a fairly inspired meal of crackers, peanut butter and strawberry jam, spanish rice mixed with nuts and jam and butter, a candy bar, and ovaltine, I burrowed into the warmth of my down bag and spent a pleasant couple of hours reading a collection of Ambrose Bierce's strange short stories.

It rained all night and through the next morning, so we did not get going until noon, just in time to catch the onset of the paddle-grabbing, boat-stopping headwind as it came up for its after-noon blow. It continued to rain and blow, off and on, for most of the day, so Forty Mile, a scant 35 miles further ahead, became the goal for the day. As I traveled, I could feel my mood balancing precariously between joy at traveling again and grumpiness at the wind and rain and at the lack of a clearly defined goal ahead to replace Dawson, slipping so slowly to the rear.

A few miles short of Forty Mile, grumpiness won out when the wind blew off a new hat that I had just bought in Dawson to replace the felt hat that I'd ruined in the Northwestern Motel laundromat. I wheeled the boat around as soon as the wind snatched the hat and managed to pass close by it just as it began to slip under the surface of the river. It is surprisingly hard to coordinate a kayak, a sinking hat, a speeding river and a gusty headwind, however, and it took me a furious second and third turn before I was back to the hat just in time to watch it dip below the opaque surface, out of reach and vision. Rich thought I had gone quite mad, belting about in circles and yelling just a bit, because he couldn't see what was taking place in the distance. Nor did he particularly care, as the rain and wind had not done wonders for his disposition either. Luckily, Forty Mile was only a mile or two further along and promised a place to set up the tents, get out of the rain, and, hopefully, regain our good spirits.

Forty Mile came into existence in 1886, when Harry Madison and Howard Franklin discovered gold on the Forty Mile River and reported their find to the 100 or so miners working the Stewart River. Most of these men immediately left their Stewart claims and headed downriver for the new field, forming the nucleus of the new community. Then, in the summer of 1887, several hundred new miners came pouring in over the Chilkoot Pass, unknowingly making a trial run for the great stampede that was to follow 11 years later.

Over the next several years the town of Forty Mile grew to become the center of supply and social life for these men, the major city to be found on the upper Yukon. The strike at Forty Mile was nowhere near the scale or richness of the Klondike, but there was still enough gold brought out of the earth to draw some remarkable enterprises to this isolated spot on the banks of the Yukon, including ten saloons, a cigar factory, a library, a dressmaker's shop and even an opera house. It was to Forty Mile that George Carmack hurried to file his claim and report his find on Rabbit Creek, and it was from Forty Mile that the citizenry rushed to set up the tent town of Dawson on the banks of the Klondike.

In its heyday, Forty Mile must have been quite a place. But as Rich and I paddled along the shore, we could see nothing but the thick green undergrowth. Finally, Rich spotted a building, quite large, set back from the shore and screened from its muddy banks by trees and the low brush. We pulled in, made fast, and quickly unloaded the boats. The building we had seen was a very large, two-story structure which had been the Mounted Police post here, before its floor rotted out and its inhabitants moved elsewhere. It was flanked by several smaller buildings, all set into an irregular clearing carpeted with foot-high ferns and tightly hemmed by the encroaching undergrowth. A narrow path or wagon road ran off about 100 yards through the overhanging foliage to a more open area containing a second cluster of buildings, including a former Customs House and a delapidated barn.

I set my tent up in front of the deserted police post, as close to the river as possible, while Rich felt the strength to carry his things 50 feet further, to set up camp among the ferns between two of the buildings. Rich wandered off to explore, as I grouchily contemplated another battle with my stove, but decided against the fray—the stove had won virtually every contest so far—and instead pulled out the small grill I was carrying. Sitting on the mossy porch of the ruined Mounty post and minding the flames

My tent in front of the RCMP post at Forty Mile.

under the grill, I created a culinary masterpiece—Noodles Romanoff, crackers with the various condiments, a cup of Postum—which helped improve my outlook and mood immeasurably.

Rich came back from his walk down the wagon trail and told me about the buildings in the second clearing and a German couple and a man named Conrad whom he had found at its other end. Rich didn't say much about Conrad—puzzling me by his inability to describe him beyond saying "He's really strange, you've got to meet him." And he didn't have to say anything about the German, as this gentleman came strolling barefooted up the overgrown trail as we were sitting watching Rich's biscuit dough rise over my fire.

The German, traveling downriver with his wife from Dawson to Eagle, sat and talked on the porch with us. He observed in a forthright European way that he wouldn't be caught dead eating the mess Rich was creating, and he offered us "some really good food you can eat" back at the cabin he and his wife were staying in, the former Forty Mile Customs House. Rich steadfastly continued to work to bring the bisquits to life, despite the German's disparaging remarks, and the man finally wandered off, prompted by his unseen wife's loud whistle. We ate the bisquits, and they proved to be quite good, well-covered with butter and jam.

Rich was full and ready for sleep, but I was neither, so I went down the path to see the buildings Rich had found and also to check on the German's food if he just happened to offer me any for comparison. I was near the Customs House when the German stuck his head out the door and called me in. Splendidly festooned with moose antlers, the Customs House is maintained by the mining companies that still work up the Forty Mile River. They use it as a place for their workers to stop overnight on their way back and forth to Dawson. The German couple had enjoyed the cabin for several days, making free use of its huge iron stove and various cooking implements. Inside I met not only the German's wife, a tall, blond and pleasant Teuton, but also Conrad.

Conrad, as Rich had described him, was indeed strange, even very freaky, but in a very agreeable way. He had an enormous, violently bushy black beard and long hair and was wearing a collage of clothing made up of bits of the original material, with patches of unrelated cloth and even strips and pieces of fur and hide here and there to fill in some of the rends and gaps. Conrad had been in Forty Mile for three weeks, staying in another cabin with his small dog, and he claimed to be floating down the river on a raft. We never saw the raft, but I wouldn't put it past Conrad

Wagon, Forty Mile.

to try the trip without one. Conrad was a happy and friendly person, and the Germans and I more or less sat back and let Conrad's novel discourse waft around and over us. It was a pleasant evening for all, especially as the German was turning out very good pear pancakes and coffee and I was enjoying a second delicious meal. We had been sitting around the table for an hour or so listening to Conrad and to the German's interesting account of a hitch hiking trip through Persia, when there was a loud tromping of boots on the boardwalk leading to the Customs House, the door was thrown violently open, and Fast Frank the Speed Demon came clomping in.

The day before we left Dawson, Rich and I had met the young man we subsequently dubbed "Speed Demon," or simply "Fast Frank." Fast Frank had come striding very purposefully up the hill of the campground across the river from the city, his slight body, crew-cut head and large ears radiating determination. Paddling unceasingly in his homemade canoe, he had reached Dawson from Whitehorse in only three or four days—as compared to our eight days—and he very seriously stated that he was traveling the length of the Yukon in five weeks as his summer's activity before starting work as a Forester in the South. Speed Demon talked casually of putting in 100 mile days as a matter of course, and he later absolutely astounded such people as the Buriens of Stewart Island and the residents of Circle, Fort Yukon, Beaver and Stevens Village by passing right by their homes and towns without even stopping. But of course such stops would slow down progress, so they were out. F.F.'s incredible speed down the river struck both Rich and myself as very funny at the time, perhaps because Frank's efforts so dwarfed and belittled ours that we *had* to find them funny in order to continue in the face of them. We had only talked briefly with Frank at that first meeting, in part because he seemed quite nervous behind his thick glasses and an enormously huge knife at his side, and he acted gruffly as a consequence.

Now Fast Frank was in our midst again, complaining that it had taken him all of seven hours to make the 55 miles from Dawson, because his boat had been stolen that morning! According to F.F., when he came down to the river to set off from Dawson, he had found his canoe missing. Luckily, the ferry pilot had seen a fellow Indian he knew towing the canoe across the river, so Frank and a helpful RCMP officer were able to retrieve his boat and all of his equipment except some food. Fast Frank remained with us in the Customs House long enough to tell his story and express astonishment, if not outright scorn, that Rich and I had taken two days to make the same distance. Then he clumped out and away, to bed down for the night and build up the energy to blast another thousand miles down the river the next day. Rich and I were both appalled that even a stolen boat had not slowed Frank down, and we wondered if such speed shouldn't receive a *real* test—perhaps a hole or two below the waterline.

Conrad and the Germans and I sat around for a while longer, enjoying the evening, the food and the diverse company. Finally I left and walked back through the forest to the tent. It was a beautiful night; the sky was clear overhead while rainclouds perched like whipped cream on the rolling hills across the now-smooth and quiet river. It was pleasant to see the sky after two days of nearly continuous rain, and I resolved to feel and travel better the next day.

My resolution was easily met on the next day's run from Forty Mile to Eagle, the first riverside community on the Alaska side of the border. The day was sunny, with a few stately cumulous clouds overhead, and although there were occasional flurries of headwind they were nothing to get upset about. I developed an excellent stroke rhythm after a bit of fussing and a few adjustments

The German and Conrad in front of the Customs House at Forty Mile.

about the boat, and then paddled the 50 miles to Eagle in seven hours. I was beginning to realize that whether a day would prove to be good or not so good seemed to depend in part on whether or not I managed to achieve a strong, continuous stroking rhythm. It was not always easy to do this, especially further down the river, and I often had to set up some sort of chant or song to keep the paddle going. Or sometimes I would contract with myself to put in 500 or 1,000 strokes before rearranging my seat or eating or taking a rest break.

One of the few stops I made that day was at the U.S.–Canadian boundary. The river below Forty Mile takes the form of seven enormous curves snaking their way toward the Alaskan border and Eagle just beyond. Mid-way through the last curve, where the river twists to the right as it flows toward the west, I came to the startling scene at the border. The high hills sloping down to the water's muddy banks have been cleared of all growth in a 30-foot swath, as if some super-sized hairclippers had shaved away the thick forest and undergrowth in a straight line from either side of the river up over the distant mountains.

I beached the kayak at the mouth of the swath on my left, in the middle of which stood a four-foot-tall obelisk which officially—and more discreetly—marked the border. I set up the tripod and took several shots of myself leaning on one side or another of this column, with the swath running up the mountain behind me. The whole while I couldn't help but wonder what Robert Ardrey, the author of *Territorial Imperative*, would have to say about the huge effort and expense that was required to set off this national boundary, which is probably seen by no more than 100 people a year.

From the boundary, it is only a few miles further on to the town of Eagle, which stands on the left bank of the river. Just before Eagle, the tight canyon walls of the river open, giving a view to the craggy snow-covered peaks standing blue with distance beyond the town. The town itself begins with scattered Indian cabins along the river bank and culminates in more substantial buildings on a high cut-bank further downriver, where the river makes a sharp turn to the right around an island. The town center is a neat little enclave, with freshly painted white buildings to give it a look of prosperity. Nestled among a number of log cabins were a well-stocked general store, a new log post office from which the mail still goes out only once a week, a prim looking white church, and a neat little airfield which runs along one side of the town center to the edge of the river. There was also Borg's Cafe, whose proprietor doubles as Customs Officer, weatherman, and god knows what else.

I went first to Borg's, of course, not only to check in with Customs I discovered that that worthy officer took care of his duty by simply nodding his head—but also to enjoy such delights as sandwiches, ice cream, cake and coffee. As I was enjoying Mrs. Borg's cooking, Rich appeared: He always seemed to know where to find me in a new community. (I fear that I am giving the impression that my trip down the Yukon was simply divided into time spent eating and time waiting to eat. That's not quite the case, but certainly the meals were an interesting part of each day, especially if they were prepared by someone else.) He joined me for the meal, and then we walked down the street to the post office and the general store.

Fast Frank clumped into the store just as we were about to leave. He retold his story of the theft of his canoe for the benefit of the sympathetic storekeeper, then set about replacing the goods that had been consumed by the thief before Speed Demon and his Mounty escort had caught up with him. Both Rich and I cringed a bit as Frank opened each order with "I don't suppose you have

The U.S. - Canadian Boundary.

Eagle.

. . ." and muttered disparagingly about "thieving Indians" as though the whole Indian Nation were in cahoots over the stealing of his canoe.

Frank certainly had reason to gripe, but his generalizations seemed grossly unreasonable and inaccurate. He also seemed to exude with every sentence the attitude that things in this region weren't really up to his standards and should be sharpened up immediately. It is perfectly understandable to have such thoughts in some parts of the world, but one's expectations have to be reasonable, and I also think that it is imperative to keep such thoughts to yourself and away from the people who live with and may even enjoy the conditions that bother you. Later, as I've said, Fast Frank dumbfounded people along the shore by going right by the major—in fact, the only—settlements on the river. It seemed that he couldn't be delayed or bothered with the people who existed along the river. All of which seemed very strange to me and absolutely mad to the people who saw him go by. But, of course, everyone is entitled to his own way, and Frank's drummer was obviously different, and much faster, than mine.

Rich and I purchased our re-supply of groceries, then walked back through the little town center, past several log homes with neat vegetable gardens running beside the log walls, to Borg's Cafe for a last cup of coffee. Then we scrambled back down the river bank to the boats and pushed off across the channel to camp on the wide sand beach of the large island that nestles in the bend of the river just across from Eagle. Fast Frank went on ahead, explaining that he ought to put in a few more miles before calling it a day.

That evening was a very slow, relaxing one. I lay on the sand on one of my sleeping mats, reading and enjoying the deepening evening. For several hours the weather was warm and the mosquitoes were elsewhere, so it was quite pleasant. Then, with a sudden buildup of dark clouds over Eagle, the air became cool and the mosquitoes suddenly returned from whatever conference they had been attending. I retired into my tent and, before sleeping, re-read the poem I had copied from a large sign nailed to the wall of one of the log homes in Eagle:

Our Town Eagle, by Harvey D. Black, M. Sgt. U.S.A., Ret.

It's mostly a bunch of tumbled down huts
And the place is overrun with Indian mutts,
And most of the grub comes packed in tins,
But it's a damn good town for the shape its in.

The weather is cold, damn cold, I'll say,
And the long winter lasts from October to May,
And most of the shacks have a roof fallen in,
But it's a damn good town for the shape its in.

The people all gossip and knock to beat hell,
And must be excused for the wild tales they tell,
And to do as they do is an unpardonable sin,
But it's a damn good town for the shape its in.

This town is divided into two social lots,
Those that are in it, and those that are not,
And knocking each other they raise a helluva din,
But it's a damn good town for the shape its in.

So there you have Eagle, as described by one of its inhabitants. Next to the poem there was a For Sale sign.

It began raining at three the next morning, June 27. I know the time fairly exactly, since I had to get up and race around in my shorts, putting up the rainfly—a waterproof sheet that ties over the tent—that I had been too lazy to set up the evening before. The tent itself isn't waterproof—can't be waterproof—since it has to be able to "breathe" away an inhabitant's perspiration. Putting on a rainfly is just enough extra work that one doesn't usually bother with it, until the rain is already drenching through the tent material.

The rain continued until two o'clock that afternoon. Even when it stopped, the grey, mean-looking clouds remained, packed low over the river, so Rich and I stayed in our tents for the day, reading and eating as the mood hit us. We would have returned to Eagle, just across the river, but because of the current it was unreachable. As it turned out, we should have bolted from the island when the rain ceased: It did not begin to rain hard again until 8:30 that evening.

As the day wore on, we both began to go a little stir-crazy, sitting in our tents. Roughly each hour, one or the other of us would yell out "Ahoy the other tent" to find out what time it was, or if the weather had cleared over on that side of the world, or simply to make some noise. At one point, during the lull in the rain, I finally crawled out and wandered around the island, but I found very little of interest other than mosquitoes and new ways of tracking more damp sand and mud back into my tent.

My tent, a Glacier brand from Sierra Designs, was billed as a two-man structure, but I found that there was only a tolerable amount of room for me and my equipment in it. Rich, by chance, had a three-man tent, also from Sierra Designs. While mine was the classic A-frame tent shape, Rich's was six-sided and conical, with three support poles that set up much faster than mine. His tent looked like a blooming cathedral alongside mine, and he had an exasperating habit of deciding aloud which portion of it he would inhabit each day. To make matters worse, his tent weighed only a little more than mine and was not that much more expensive. You could cut the envy that pervaded the narrow confines of my little orange affair as I listened to Rich doing wind-sprints or practicing his tumbling in his!

A constant, drizzling, boring rain continued through our second night on the island across from Eagle. I set the alarm for four and poked my head out of the tent in the hope of finding everything clear and calm outside. It wasn't, so I repeated the experiment again at five, six and seven, but with no discernable change. I breakfasted on something or other and tried to read some more, but as the morning wore on I was beginning to have the same trapped, claustrophobic feelings I had known three weeks earlier, when I was caught behind the ice on Bennett Lake. By noon, after remaining in the tent for 36 hours, I could stand it no longer and decided to get back onto the river regardless of the conditions. At this point it had rained continuously for the last 16 hours, and for all I knew it might never stop. I "ahoyed" Rich and found that he, too, was more than ready to move on.

Outside, we found the rain had slackened, although a heavy wind was slicing along up the river, and fog banks stood like filmy walls over the water, suspended from a roof of dense low cloud. No matter. Down came the tents, the boats were loaded, and we were off. Or, at least, almost off. During our stay on the island, the river level had dropped about ten inches, which meant that our boats, pulled just out of the water two days before, now sat 20 feet from the water's edge. It took several minutes of shoving and pulling to get them back into their element.

By two o'clock, when everything was finally ready to go, the rain had started coming down with greater determination. But it was good to be active after two days, and I was reasonably happy as I traveled through the rain, the wind-whipped waves and the shifting fog banks. I fell into a good paddling rhythm, stroking along below the surrounding mountainous hills that looked like hump-backed dinosaurs sleeping in the mists until the sun returned to awaken them to violent battle. Twelve miles from Eagle I passed Calico Bluff on the left. Tremendous geological forces have rippled and tumbled the strata exposed by the downward-cutting river, so that they now look almost like a child's swirling design in finger paints. The bluff looked ancient and black in the rain, tortured but impervious under the rolling clouds.

The rain and wind made this day's travel on the river a very chill, damp affair. I became quite cold, despite the exercise and several layers of clothing topped by a rainproof slicker. Rich, who won't wear a waterproof covering because it doesn't "breathe," was drenched through his water-repellent parka and was shivering almost uncontrollably when I slowed to let him catch up with me. He was very anxious to stop, so we pulled into a spot marked on the map as Millers Camp, 25 miles from Eagle, hoping to find a serviceable cabin there. Instead, we found only thick mud and mosquitoes, voracious hordes of them.

We moved on, driven back to our boats by the mosquitoes; but shortly after Millers, Rich simply pulled his boat to shore on a sloping sand spit and began to unload. I remained in the kayak, the rain dripping off me, watching Rich's boots sink into the damp sand and mud of the bank. I felt wet and cold, but it certainly looked far worse out on that sand bank. And I really felt that today's was still too short an effort. After all, it might continue raining for weeks. I told Rich that I was going to continue on and try to reach the abandoned site of Nation, 20 miles or so down the river. Tired, cold and discouraged, Rich hardly turned his head as I paddled away.

It rained all that afternoon, but a good paddling rhythm carried me the distance to Nation fairly rapidly. At one point along the way, I spotted a moose cow and calf grazing in the mist at the edge of an island. I tried to take a photograph, which did not come out well; but, nonetheless, it was fun sitting there for a few minutes watching the two rather preposterous creatures moving calmly about the island in the midst of the downpour. Several hours later, I reached the point where Nation was supposed to be located but found nothing visible along the shore. However, just beyond the vacant site, I spotted a very nice little cove set into a low island, a perfect spot to pull the boat in and set up camp. I hastily threw up the tent, gathered my things inside, changed into dry clothing and set about trying to prepare dinner—which, yes indeed, meant dealing with my mechanical nemesis again.

I'll spare you the horrid details, simply saying that the bloody stove declined to function after almost an hour of patient coaxing. I was on the point of tearing it to shreds with my bare hands when I heard a whoop from outside. I peered out of the tent and was amazed to see Rich roaring down the river toward my campsite. He beached his canoe and explained that he had set up his tent, cooked a meal, changed his clothes, and then decided that he also hadn't really put in enough miles. So he dismantled everything again and set out after me.

As soon as Rich had his tent up again, we entered into stiff negotiations wherein I gained the use of his stove in return for providing him with a second dinner. It all worked out very well, and we spent the next hour in his capacious tent, listening to the endless rain endlessly dripping down outside, feasting on a meal of rice and hash and jello pudding.

The next morning it was still raining. I just could not, or did not want to, believe it. The rainfall had continued now for 48 hours, with a break of only five hours the day before. And it seemed perfectly ready to continue for another 48 days. To add insult to injury, the sun was shining strongly enough through the clouds and rain to cast shadows. We finally returned to the river at noon —in the rain, of course; but there was no question now of not traveling. Nothing short of a blizzard could have kept me cooped up in that tent for another day.

We were enjoying a slackening in the rain, in sight of a landmark called Biederman Bluff some 20 miles downriver from Nation, when we both spotted Fast Frank's red canoe, looking strangely askew and abandoned on a rocky beach to our right. We found ourselves wondering if Speed Demon might have gotten into some sort of difficulty, especially as we would have expected him to be hundreds of miles further down the river by now. We paddled over and beached our boats, discovering with some relief that Frank's canoe was tied up and intact. There was a path of sorts cut into the high bank facing the river, so we walked up, wondering where Frank might be.

We found him in a cabin on the tree-filled flat above, happily cooking soup over a roaring stove. The cabin belonged to a man who lived in Eagle, and a sign by the door invited anyone's use so long as they replaced the kindling. Frank had found the cabin early the day before, and he had finally decided to rest for a day and escape the rain. He admitted that he was beginning to wonder if he would actually be able to finish the 1,200 miles of Yukon that still lay ahead of him in the four weeks or so that he had left, but he also firmly asserted that he was going to beat out "a hundred miles or so to Circle" the following day. We congratulated Frank once again on his indomitable energy, then said goodbye and paddled around the next bend of the river, where we found a good sandbar the hard way—by almost getting caught up in the shallows which sloped off from its flank.

We spread out our tarps on the damp sand for dinner, and as we sat there munching down our various bits of food—in my case, cheese and jerky on crackers with butter, oatmeal, and tea with honey—a very wonderful thing happened. Orchestrated by the quiet flowing sounds of the river at our feet, the clouds slowly danced apart and the sun came out. Then, for the first time in three days, the cloud cover lifted, and we had our first glimpse of the rugged peaks lining the horizon to the south—white snow clutched at the tips of up-thrust rocky fingers. After days of confinement to narrow corridors of vision bounded by either tent walls or slightly more removed grey cloud walls, what a pleasure it was to be able to look off into the newly revealed distances through the evening sun's rays slanting brightly past the remaining clouds.

The pleasant mood produced by this abrupt change in weather continued and expanded after I got back into the Quisnam and began paddling downriver. As the evening deepened, it became the most beautiful I had yet experienced on the river. At one point, the sun slid behind a wide band of thunderclouds drifting through the sky, and the hills and larger mountains marching toward the horizon stood out in gunmetal-blue relief against the setting sun. The river was smooth enough to reflect these blue-black hills, then a band of gold reflected from the hidden sun, and finally the deeply shadowed, white and black, gilt-edged cloud floating overhead. Behind me, a great sweep of empty blue sky rushed down to meet a billowing tower of pure white cumulonimbus cloud standing high on the horizon and reflecting the setting sun like a gigantic movie screen. In that direction the lands and hills surrounding the river caught the sun and were green and lush in its embrace, counterpointing the complex, vaporous spire beyond.

I felt myself soaring with the spectacular scene, and I easily stroked out another 20 miles to a campsite beneath the canyon walls near Woodchopper Creek. The tents went up in another agreeable site on the upper end of a small island; and despite the clouds that slowly began to close in overhead, Rich and I struck a note of defiance against the weather of the past few days by not putting up the rainflys. We shouldn't have been so bold. At 2:30 the next morning I was back outside again, dancing around in shorts and bare feet to get the rainfly up between me and the pouring heavens. It proved to be largely a false alarm, however; the next morning dawned warm and wonderfully, incredibly, ecstatically sunny.

You wouldn't believe the orgy of sunning, washing, cleaning and drying that took place on that sand beach that morning. We reveled in and absorbed the warm morning sunshine, like dry sponges returned to water. After washing myself—my first bath since Dawson nine days before—I shook or washed the sand out of everything and rearranged the Quisnam from the helter-skelter conditions produced by several days of simply throwing everything in and jumping in after. The sun continued to shine down around clouds that were cottony and attractive, not grey and bellicose. And to make this paradise perfect, nary a mosquito made an appearance throughout.

Once we got underway, I paddled energetically through the first part of the late morning and early noon, looking for a stream and some clear drinking water. Finally I found exactly what I was hoping for, a brook tumbling clear and cold directly down a rocky wall into the river. I drank and refilled my plastic water bottles, then set off again. But my energy seemed to extend only this far and no further: Beyond the stream I found myself quite happy simply to sit back and drift along the river. It was a nice way to pass the miles, counting the trees and keeping track of the clouds overhead.

As the canyons about the river opened back into flatter land again, I spotted two children standing by the shore a few hundred yards ahead. I decided that it wouldn't do to let these two see anything but an indomitably rugged and energetic kayaker passing by, so I went back to work briefly, paddling vigorously toward them. As I neared the boys, about eight and twelve years of age, I asked them if they lived here. They said that they did, in a cabin hidden in the trees behind them, and that their parents both trapped in the winter. The oldest boy let me know that he also would be going out trapping in the next year or so. Before our conversation was forced to an end by distance, I learned that they had their schooling right there at home through a correspondence course run by a midwestern university—a means of education quite common along the river.

As I left them, I wondered what sort of a life it must be for these two boys, and the few like them, who grow up here in the river wilderness. What vistas of experience, of self-reliance before truly dangerous surroundings (including winter temperatures of -50 degrees) these boys must encounter on their journey to adulthood. Here were two little boys, playing by the river on a summer's day, already knowledgeable about the natural world that surrounds them in a way that the rest of us, who grow up in the midst of our urban concrete and "comforts," will never know. What a sensational experience. And of course they must take it all for granted, and very probably wish that they might live in the cities they have heard so much about.

Further along the river, the nice fluffy white clouds drifting above me suddenly coalesced into a mighty, turbulent thunderhead directly over the river ahead of us. Torrents of rain were streaming down, so both Rich and I wearily secured our boats again. A stiff headwind forced us back to paddling to keep moving forward, but the thundercloud, so ominous, proved to be a paper tiger (paper torrent?) as far as we were concerned; for it drifted past and its rain never touched us. The sun returned as we stroked around a curve and a final long and steep rocky canyon wall into the first truly different countryside to be seen along the river since Lake LaBerge, 700 miles behind. On our left, and out ahead, lay the Yukon Flats. We were ten miles from Circle, and as we paddled toward that small town the land all around dropped down, down, until nothing could be seen on the horizon but trees on the waterline and blue sky above.

15   The Flats, Part I: The City of Circle
and the Oil Business

The Yukon Flats are a gigantic curving basin 250 miles long and 10 to 40 miles wide, stretching from just above Circle to just below Stevens Village. Here there are no mountains, no mounds, no rock, nothing higher on the horizon than thick growths of scraggily spruce and dense alder and willow brush that top the thousands and thousands of low, shifting sand and gravel islands that clot the river without end. The main channel of the river is a mad array of islands, and peripheral sloughs may stretch for 40 miles through the low tundra, their waters still and dead, traps for the unwary and lost. The river drops less than 300 feet through the Flats, only a little over a foot a mile.

A map of the Flats is a wonder to behold. The Yukon twists and turns like a thing demented, but it is straight in comparison with some of the smaller tributary streams that twist aimlessly and endlessly across the maps and the corresponding flat tundra. The names on the maps are eloquent testimony to what travel on the Flats can be like—names like Crazy Slough, Dead Man's Island, Halfway Whirlpool and the townsite of Purgatory. Where the Flats don't carry twisting rivers and streams, they hold near-stagnant lakes, thousands of them, which combine to make this area one of the greatest bird sanctuaries (and mosquito breeding grounds) on this planet.

Several years ago, an ambitious plan was presented by the Army Corps of Engineers for the creation of a dam in Rampart Canyon, beyond the lower end of the Flats, to produce a gigantic inland lake over all this area and a source of electricity beyond Alaska's wildest needs. Such a plan undoubtedly embodies a typical human reaction to the Flats: "Let's *drown* the bloody place." But it was a senseless plan, when one considers the natural habitat that would be destroyed and the useless lake that would be produced in its place. Luckily the plan was shelved as a result of public outcry and the discovery that Rampart Canyon lacked the deep solid rock necessary for adequately anchoring the dam. The Flats remain in all their bizarre splendor, waiting to provide days of unusual experience for the traveler coming down the river.

Perhaps the most unique aspect of traveling in the Flats is that you find yourself instantly disoriented, lost beyond all help, as soon as you round the bend away from whatever town or village you are leaving. The islands that choke the Yukon here are forever changing before the force of the river, and I defy anyone to keep accurate track of where they are. A pot-bellied former trapper in Circle assisted our departure from that village with the observation "Any fool can know where he is in the Flats if he just watches his map." Baloney. I didn't know where I was ten minutes after leaving him, despite having the appropriate map spread out before me the whole time. There is nothing to sight against in the Flats, no rise or promontory to grasp at as a reference point. You might as well be out on the ocean or in the Sahara Desert.

So how do you get through the Flats? To travel here, you must .be calm, content to let the river, God, the fates, carry you along the way. Surprisingly, luckily, there is quite a strong current running through the main channel in the Flats, like a string laid out through a great maze, and it is this current that will lead you through if you will just let it. If you paddle indiscriminantly, you will lose the way, because when you give propulsion to your craft, you can't tell where the river's current is going. And it is foolhardy to attempt to sight a course through the islands with map and compass, because the current and the channel it runs through seem never to have heard of system and logic. When you see a long open waterway heading in what seems to be the right direction through the islands ahead, you can be sure that the thread of current will swing you to the left around this island, then back to the right through that narrow channel—in fact, in any direction except down that obvious open avenue. If the Puritan Ethic for work proves simply too strong, you can paddle along the sides of the islands, where the current has no place to turn, but then you must stop at the ends of the islands to discover the next course of the river, or you risk getting yourself off into still water or back up a slough from which it might take days or even weeks to extricate yourself.

Actually, traveling on the Flats proved to be great fun. I would get up in the morning, load the boat, paddle energetically out from whatever island or sandspit I had been camping on, then put down my paddle, rest my feet on the deck of the kayak, and float along enjoying the passing scenery while reading a few pages of a book, in this case Thoreau. I also paddled occasionally, especially toward the end of the Flats, when I may have gotten myself

Sunset on the Flats.

off into a side channel. But I spent a fair amount of time in the nearly supine position described, and I quite enjoyed it.

The Flats were everywhere exactly the same, but also, of course, amazingly varied and different. There were islands, islands beyond count, but each island had its own shape, its own vegetation, to make it unique and worthy of some attention. Overhead there were clouds changing shape constantly—at times being the little cotton balls of fair weather, at times stacking themselves into soaring cumulonimbus clouds that walked the earth nearby and miles away on gigantic black pillars of rain. And everywhere the birds existed in profusion, flying and swimming and nesting on the many islands. The whole immense basin seemed constructed to force the hurrying traveler to slow down, sit back, and contemplate an intricate biosphere of island and tree and bird and animal, pierced and flooded by a mighty river, resting almost directly on the Arctic Circle. Although at times I got quite tired of the Flats, especially at that point near the end where I may have lost the main channel, in fact the Flats stand out as a portion of the trip I highly value, a completely different experience from what had gone before or was to come after.

The touring company of "Rich and I" paddled out from under the rain clouds on that afternoon of June 30 and continued down the river and up a little side channel to the town of Circle, so named bacause it was believed—mistakenly—to lie within the Arctic Circle (it is actually 50 miles below). The town was founded in 1894, after two Indians, grubstaked by Jack McQuesten, discovered gold on Birch Creek nearby. McQuesten, the founder of Fort Reliance and general storekeeper for much of the upper Yukon during those years, came down from Forty Mile to establish a store for the new community. Over the next 12 years the population of Circle rose to more than 1,000, and the gold production from the nearby creeks amounted to over a million dollars a year. Circle, being well within the Alaskan boundary, offered ruggedly individualistic mining men and prospectors relief from the careful regulation and control exerted by the Mounted Police in Canada, and many flocked to this wide open town because of that. But the town nearly ceased to exist when word came downriver of a new and far richer strike at some place called the Klondike, in the winter of 1896–97. The town became depopulated overnight, and valuable properties and buildings instantly became worthless, unwanted.

Today, Circle is dominated by a single building, the Yukon Trading Post. This building, a three-year-old, one-story structure of shiny new logs and aluminum roofing, is owned by Frank Warren and his family, who have run the Trading Post for the past 12 years. Their new building houses the town's store, its post office, the government liquor store, a cafeteria, and what may be the town's sole communications center. The little town, home for about a dozen whites and perhaps 50 Indians, is quite prosperous, primarily because of the tourists who drive up the Steese Highway, which ends at the town, and then fly (in a plane owned and operated by the Warren family, I believe) on to Fort Yukon in order to be able to say that they have been inside the Arctic Circle. Also, since Fort Yukon, with its 800 thirsty inhabitants, is officially "dry," there is a constant flow of riverboats through the Flats to Circle to pick up necessary refreshment.

Although Rich and I could hear a noisy pump for miles, we had to be practically on the shores of the town before we caught any sight of Circle. We landed at a low sandspit just across from the town and thought to make camp there until we stepped out onto the low sandbar. Water oozed up from the sand, and Rich, with a little in-place treading on the highest point of the little island, quickly sank in up to his knees. We settled for dinner

The Yukon Flats.

there, safe from the noise and hub-bub radiating from Circle a few hundred yards away, then paddled across to the town and beached the boats just down from a small public campground. Our maneuvers were closely watched by a silent group of men who stood on the high ground above us, inspecting us as though we were on parade.

For some reason I'd pictured quite a metropolis here, and during the first few minutes in Circle I had to make some considerable adjustments to condense my image of the business district into the actuality of a single store. We set up our tents in the campground, then walked up to the store to look around. Since the day was June 30, only four days short of the Fourth of July, four or five over-anxious teenage kids were already shattering the possible peace of the area with firecrackers and an occasional impromptu dash about the dirt streets of the town aboard an old truck. I rather like firecrackers myself, but I found the explosions less than wonderful when they continued late into the night, as Rich and I and eight or ten others in the small campground tried to sleep through the racket. Later, about three in the morning, we were all disturbed again by an even greater onslaught—a party of absolute barbarians, real Neanderthal dolts, who drove up to the campground in two cars, leapt out yelling to one another and at a barking dog, set off firecrackers, and noisily dumped two boats into the water in preparation for a race into the wilderness to blast anything that moved. One drunken fool boasted to his friends and to anyone else within five miles about the damage two shots from his revolver had done to somebody's window and to a ground squirrel that had unwisely crossed his path. If thoughts could kill, I'm sure these louts would have been burned in their tracks by the silent and suffering people trying to sleep all around them.

Since I'd been up earlier to check on the safety of the boats when some young boys were playing with rocks down by the water, I told Rich that it was his turn this time, and he grumbled out of his tent to make sure the baboons didn't make as free with our means of transportation as they were with our sleep. He told me later that of the group, one man, who appeared to be the father of several of the others, seemed to be quite reasonable and sane—that is, until he set off from the shore with each hand on a control stick of two enormously oversized outboard motors, evidently trying to get the boat to fly.

About seven the next morning, the sun streaming down on the walls of my tent made it too hot for further residence, so I got up and wandered around the still-sleeping town. At one point I found myself talking with a man from Fairbanks who had a small but very neat houseboat tied up on the river. He talked for a while about the small cabin he owned near Nation, which he had left open and stocked for anyone needing shelter, until it had been stripped clean of everything that might be moved. He blamed hippies going down the river on rafts, but he also had some choice criticisms for our red-neck visitors of the night before. The man was rough-hewn, tall and very weathered, but he spoke well, even captivatingly. I found myself enjoying his conversation both then and later, when Rich and I were having coffee in the cafeteria. He was an electrician by trade, and he said that he spent most of his leisure hours with his wife and children in short jaunts on the river in his small houseboat. I occasionally found myself objecting to, or at least wondering about, some of his assertions, such as his complaint about hippies wrecking his cabin, but I kept such thoughts to myself. It seems best, if you want to find out what a person thinks—and especially if you have just met them and probably won't see them again—to just keep nodding and listening and privately evaluating what they have to say.

To pass the morning, at least until the town woke up a bit more, I caught up on some of my writing, then engaged in another

Rich.

conversation with a young man and woman who asked to look over one of my topo maps to see where they should fish on Birch Creek, a very sinuous stream that runs parallel to the Yukon behind Circle. The girl turned out to be the previous year's teacher in the small village of Rampart, 350 miles downriver, and she asked me to tell the kids there that "Big Smith" said hello. She was a gorgeous girl (funny how almost every girl seen on this trip seemed to qualify as "gorgeous"; could it have anything to do with being on the river for days and even weeks at a time without seeing one?).

She happened to mention that her father had spent the last two summers conducting a canoe, alone, along the Arctic coast of Alaska and Canada to film what he found there. Such an exploit truly puts my small trip down the Yukon into perspective. (Another exploit I heard about, from a young man in Tanana who knew them, was that of two men who went by kayak down the MacKenzie River, *up* the Rat, and down the Bell, Porcupine and lower Yukon for a total of 6,000 miles in four or five months. That *really* puts my 1,200 miles in a month or so into its proper place.) "Big Smith" also impressed upon me the fact of there being a close community of people along the river, despite the hundreds of miles that separate many of its members. She cited the number of Circle residents who knew of her and spoke to her because of her radio conversations from Rampart the winter before.

Rich and I finally managed to get ourselves going, loading the boats up between sessions of coffee and food at the cafeteria and pushing off into the warm sun on the Yukon by about noon. This was one of the best departures of the trip, as two groups of tourists, one a young couple, the other an older couple being shown around Alaska by their in-laws, hovered about us as we prepared to set out, asking numerous questions about our trip, taking pictures, and exclaiming among themselves about how brave we surely were. It was all great fun, and we both were guilty of putting in a little extra flourish of paddle as we pulled away from shore. We also concentrated very hard on paddling a straight and rapid line away from Circle and around the nearest bend, since the old pot-bellied trapper with such great faith in the maps of the Flats had said "Most people leave here going sideways" and was now standing on the bank above the river and watching our departure very carefully. As soon as we got around the corner of an island and out of sight, we immediately collapsed on our paddles and drifted for the next ten minutes, catching our breath.

To our surprise, and joy, once we got away from Circle and out into the main channel, we found a quite reasonable current there to carry us along. Without it, as I have said earlier, we could never have threaded our way through the maze of islands. The day became a fascinating spectator event, as we drifted here and there among the islands on a most illogical and surprising course. During the first few hours we made futile attempts to double-check our location with map and compass, but after that we abandoned all such efforts and simply put all our faith in the current.

A few minutes from Circle, we had to pass under a tall giant of a cloud, black and angry, but it withheld its rain. After that we drifted with the current under clouds like small rolls of perfectly white cotton scattered about the sky. The sun was warm throughout the day, the warmest of the trip so far, and for the first time I had to travel in just a tennis shirt to be comfortable. I also traveled barefoot throughout the day rather than have my feet melting inside rubber boots. I was pleased to discover that I could cross my feet inside the kayak this way, opening up quite a variety of new positions to keep myself comfortable while riding for long hours.

Circle City.

We stopped for dinner a million miles from Circle, or so it seemed, on a low and round gravel island surrounded by other, more substantial plots of gravel and brush. And here something straight out of Hitchcock's "The Birds" occurred. I was walking a short distance from the kayak, just looking around, when an Arctic tern, a bird with white feathers and black head cowl, suddenly buzzed me, turned, and screeching hoarsely, dived at me again and again. By moving into its territory I'd set off some sort of attack command, and the poor bird seemed willing to wheel and dive unendingly until I departed. I spent quite a few minutes trying to capture the bird on film as it rocketed by, and then after a brief search, I found the nest it was trying to protect, a little depression in the gravel surrounded by a few twigs and holding two small mottled-brown eggs. It seemed a shame to work this poor bird any more—especially in light of its having made a 12,000-mile migration from Antarctica to Africa to this spot on the Yukon in order to nest. I quickly went back to my supper and left the bird in peace.

While in Circle we had noticed some huge blue tractors pulled up in a field near the Warren's store. We were told that they belonged to an oil search firm. Now, from our island, we spotted more of the tractors about a half mile away on a bluff above the river. Both Rich and I were curious about the plans and proceedings of the oil company—and we were also interested in finding out roughly where we were—so a few minutes after setting out from our dinner island, we guided the boats to the base of a steep dirt bank and clambered up with the help of several hands stretched down from above.

One of the men helping us to the top of the crumbling bank was Bob Sealy, a huge and craggy man of about 50 who was in charge of the many hundreds of thousands of dollars worth of equipment that now stood silent, waiting to be carried by barge to Circle and then elsewhere. Sealy introduced himself and the four other men who were there to help him transfer the equipment —several large tractors and many truck-trailer sized structures mounted on tractor treads—and explained that it all belonged to the United Geophysical Corporation, which had been hired by Texaco the winter before to search this portion of the Flats for indications of oil. Sealy also introduced us to a young couple, the Delman Halls of Pleasant Hill, California, who had arrived at this small point of land just the day before, on their trip by canoe from Eagle to Fort Yukon. The Halls had been enjoying the open-handed hospitality of the men of United Geophysical. Small wonder—Mrs. Hall was another of those gorgeous women that I kept meeting on the river.

One of the men with Sealy insisted that Rich and I really needed some sort of decent anchor for our boats while we were visiting, so he backed a hulking D-9 Caterpillar tractor to the edge of the river for the purpose. Convinced of the security of our boats, we followed Sealy back to the small community of tracked structures for a cup of coffee. These wagons were lined up in a double row, some made up as bunk houses, while the one we climbed into was fitted as a kitchen and small dining hall. There we got not only a cup of coffee but a second complete meal of chicken and mashed potatoes produced by the genial bare-chested cook whose name, most appropriate for this part of the world, was Howard Mosquito.

As we ate, Sealy sat at our table, leaning back in his chair and talking with us about his massive operation in the wilds of the Yukon Flats. He explained that the United Geophysical Corporation is an oil search company which rents its talents and men and equipment to whichever oil company requires their services. Before this assignment for Texaco, Sealy's firm was involved in the rich discoveries beneath Prudhoe Bay on the Arctic Slope of Alaska.

Attack of the Arctic tern.

Their method of operation is incredibly expensive but surprisingly simple. Once winter has come to freeze the rivers and put down a deep and solid covering of snow over the land, the search begins. The tractors mounted with enormous blades go out first, cutting a path through the trees that extend above the snow level. Behind these first tractors come others, pulling the wagons filled with all the comforts possible in a climate in which the winter temperatures are normally 50 or 60 degrees below zero. The purpose of all this activity is to bring in intricate equipment that tests for oil by sending and receiving seismic waves through the ground. The findings, spewed out by a computer aboard one of the wagons, are immediately grabbed, deciphered and hidden by a representative of Texaco. For, of course, if a major strike should be made, Texaco would want as few outside people as possible to know about it.

All of these wagons are pulled along, testing as they go, in relentlessly straight lines for miles over the frozen tundra. However, when the long entourage comes to a river, it makes a careful little button-hook before crossing, so that people passing down the waterway during the summer will not have their views ruined by a broad phantom highway stretching endlessly away through the trees of the Flats. According to Sealy, a normal day's effort saw three to five miles of advance over the frozen Flats, for which United Geophysical was paid by the mile.

The operation entails enormous operating expenses. Planes fly into this massive exploration effort up to three times a day, landing on strips bulldozed into the snow, bringing food, oil, equipment and whatever new personnel are needed. The men work eight to ten hours a day, but the equipment is kept running all the time to prevent it from freezing. It is hard to imagine the difficulty of working in conditions in which touching metal with bare flesh will mean the loss of most of that flesh and a man's spit will freeze with a crackling pop long before it hits the ground. It is easy to imagine the millions of dollars that such an expedition must cost the sponsoring oil company. I wonder if Texaco found anything?

Sealy was careful to explain that he himself knew nothing about the scientific side of the operation he managed. Yet his accurate explanations of how those details were handled suggested otherwise. He also seemed to become happiest when he was talking about his work at Prudhoe Bay. He didn't say too much about it, but he did allow as how he and the rest of his crew knew—despite the secrecy—that something was up as they probed into that greatest of recent oil discoveries.

We were invited to stay in one of the bunkhouse wagons for the night, but Rich seemed to want to go on, and I realized that our conversation with the people of United Geophysical had been of exactly the right length. It is nice to depart from friends, even new-found friends, while you are still enjoying their company, rather than after the first bloom of meeting has worn off. (I'm giving away the fact that I seem to like people, almost any people, in short doses.) Bob Sealy's hospitality represented almost the first I received on the river and, as it turned out, almost the last. I was glad to have met this craggy, soft-spoken man.

The sun was low in the sky by now, dutifully doing its job of painting the evening clouds and the river surface into a splendid blend of burnished copper and gold. In leaving the shore, I spun the boat back into the current with an extra swirl and flourish, waving grandly to the men and to Mrs. Hall while working energetically to keep myself upright. We camped on another shallow gravel island an hour downriver and fell asleep with the sound of the river in our ears, burbling as it swirled past an outstretched arm of the island.

16   The Flats, Part II:Fort Yukon and Beyond

I woke the next morning, that of July 2, to find that the river's level had once again gone way up. The kayak, beached the night before, was completely afloat and tugging at the line holding it to a sun-bleached log; I made a mental note to tether it even more carefully. I looked up from the floating kayak to find the morning sky brightly blue and absolutely clear of any clouds. The sun was warm, the Flats quiet and endless, the river smooth and glistening. The only flaw in the beautiful morning was the phalanx of horseflies which had been following us since Circle, and now picked us up again as we began to travel. Unlike the mosquitoes, these equally cursed pests had the strength and speed to stay with the boats traveling on the river, and nothing other than a lucky bash into oblivion seemed to drive them away. The horseflies didn't do anything, which was perhaps their most irritating characteristic; they simply buzzed around you, hour after hour, until you were ready for mayhem.

The fine weather and the fascination of another day's travel through the Flats, wondering where the current might carry the boats next, kept the annoyance of the flies in perspective. Our destination was Fort Yukon, a village of 500 people, mostly Indians, and the largest city on the Alaskan portion of the Yukon. The area in which Fort Yukon stands was first explored by John Bell, and the fort itself was constructed in 1847 by Alexander Hunter Murray, both men working as employees of the Hudson's Bay Company. Fort Yukon owes its situation to the Porcupine River, which meets the Yukon as its major tributary in a maze of islands a mile below the townsite. The Porcupine has its start in Canada, where it offered a natural highway for exploration by members of the H.B.C., which had long been established on the not-too-distant MacKenzie River. Fort Yukon was actually well inside Russian territory, but the trappers and traders of the Hudson's Bay Company didn't let that stop their creation of a booming fur trade. In any case, the Russians never bothered the fort, and it was the Americans in 1869 who finally firmly requested that the Hudson's Bay Company remove itself from the newly purchased American soil.

Our journey to Fort Yukon was even more bewildering and seemingly aimless than yesterday's from Circle. At one point the current carried us rapidly between several islands, then abruptly died out as we coasted directly toward another island barring our way. We threaded our way past several more islands and then were suddenly picked up by the current and on our way again. At another point Rich went one way around an island with the current, while a low sandbar guided me off in another direction. I didn't see Rich again for more than an hour, as I worked my way around this island and that. But then, as I paddled out of a still slough I'd inexplicably drifted into, I burst back into the main channel and found myself ahead of him.

As we neared Fort Yukon we spotted two enormous and very out-of-place radar towers poking up over the trees fringing the riverbank. A few minutes later, we crossed the Arctic Circle—there was no discernable difference in the lush green vegetation from one side to another—and pulled up on a spit of land that lies just above the town, separated from it by a long dead-end tongue of still water. The point of land offered a small clearing carpeted in foot-high ferns and backed by the usual thick, ten-foot-high shrubbery and trees. The water was very high here, practically level with the flat fern meadow, so that we had only to step a few inches up from our boats in the river to be on the level with our tents.

Looking north from the spit, I could see that the town of Fort Yukon was strung along a road running from a cluster of large gas or oil storage tanks and a few two-story buildings fronting the river, back along the dead-end slough toward the two radar towers which rose out of the trees a half mile away on the right. I set up camp, then guided the empty kayak up the narrow dead-end channel, looking at the small log cabins fronting the water on the bank above me. The larger buildings at the upper end of town turned out to be a school and what I believe was called an Indian Culture Center, and a short walk up from the boat between these structures put me on the long main street of Fort Yukon, which paralleled the slough.

The dusty street was lined in a haphazard way with small tree-shaded cabins and was busy with the comings and goings of a multitude of Indian children. Seeing that a number of these kids were nibbling various goodies as they came out of what looked like a slightly larger cabin, I instantly changed direction for the cabin and entered it, to find a general store hidden inside. The storekeeper, a Filipino woman, sold me a very small bag of essentials, such as Screaming Yellow Zonkers, for $12, assuring me that her's were the lowest prices in town. They weren't, with margarine at 69 cents, peanut butter at $1.35, and 1½ pounds of jelly at $2, but these prices were only a few cents more than those in the other stores in town. Food is *expensive* in the north.

I walked back to the boat, put my bag of groceries behind the seat, and paddled back down the slough, watching the Indians watching me as they walked and worked on the cabin-lined bluff above the shore. One youngster standing on a small ledge of dirt below the high riverbank walls whipped around when he heard me paddling by and grinned sheepishly at me: I think he was doing something appropriately boyish and horrid to some of the occupants of the many swallow's nests in the bank.

I continued beyond the slough to the river and the lower end of Fort Yukon, where I beached the boat again, making one of my sloppier and wetter landings: I not only had to fight the current, but also had to work the kayak around behind a large riverboat anchored to the shore where I wanted to stop. All of this would not have mattered a great deal, except that my landing was performed under the watchful eyes of several Fort Yukon residents. (I'm not sure that I have ever described a neat landing fully, but I *had* learned to beach the kayak fairly well under normal conditions. For some reason, it proved easiest when in fast current to pick the desired point on the shore as it came toward me, then as the boat was just about beside that point, to paddle hard on the outside, backpaddle on the inside, and push the rudder pedal for a hard turn in the direction of the shore. Done correctly, the boat would turn about in a smooth swirl so that it faced the shore slightly but was also pointed partly upstream. Then I would paddle hard against the current, and if all went well, the boat would end by pointing exactly up river at the moment its side touched the shore. All of this extra activity was required because I found that if I tried simply to nose into shore with the current still carrying me forward, the boat tended to cartwheel around anyway and I would have far less control over it.)

I walked along a path running through the dense brush to the main center of town. There was a small hotel here with a closed cafe, a large Alaska Commercial Company store, and the beginning of the long street that held the school and community center a quarter of a mile away. Another street running at right angles to the first led by the post office and another store to the Fort Yukon airport. I checked into the two stores at this end of Fort

Our camp at Fort Yukon.

Yukon (the prices, as I've noted, were lower than the first store), then picked up some mail at the post office and walked out to the airport.

There was a great deal of activity on the dirt runway and standing area, because fire-fighting crews were working over a PBY that was being used to water-bomb a blaze near Circle. In Alaska, only those fires threatening towns or otherwise valuable areas are fought. The rest are simply allowed to burn themselves out. However, this policy still leaves plenty of work for native Alaskan fire-fighting teams. I walked to the terminal of the airport, a small office attached to a warehouse filled with mail-order merchandise, and asked some questions about the cost of flying out with my equipment from some of the towns further down the Yukon.

I had no idea how far down the river I was finally going to go. Whenever anyone asked, I always said "I'll be happy if I can get to Tanana." Now Tanana was only 330 miles ahead, and I found myself looking on down the river, toward Nulato, which I hoped might be an Eskimo village. (In fact, the Eskimo do not extend very far up the Yukon, which I did not know at this point. Their first village lies at least 600 miles beyond Fort Yukon.) After getting some answers from the young man running the desk in the terminal, and after musing over the large sign that said the terminal was

"Absolutely Not Responsible" for any alcoholic beverages left on the premises (remember, Fort Yukon was supposed to be dry), I walked back along the hot and dusty Fort Yukon streets to the river, and then along the narrow trail through the shrubbery to the kayak.

I was determined to make a very graceful exit from where the boat was tied up, because I was still being observed by the people who had seen my poor docking effort of a few minutes earlier; it was just my luck that they would take an interest in someone in a kayak pulling to shore in their back yard. Imbued with my new resolve, I very carefully knocked off my camera lens cap as I put another small bag of groceries into the boat, neatly flicking the cap into the water just by the edge of the shore, where it shelved steeply under the water. Which of course meant that the cap was gone forever, hidden under the opaque surface. Maintaining my iron control and calm, I smoothly entered the boat, merely getting both feet wet and nearly tipping it over in the process. Then, to drive home the point I was making, I paddled off against the current looking like a broken-winged duck trying to fly. Since one of the rudder lines had managed to come loose again, I was forced to hack away at the water on only one side to offset the way the uncontrolled rudder was trying to turn the boat. I feel certain that I produced a memorable performance of grace and control for my appreciative spectators.

The little fern meadow by the side of the river was quite hot, even with the sun lowering, so I strung up my tarp as a shade and settled down to make a superb meal of Yellow Zonkers, Kool Aid and a can of Sloppy Joe. After some thought, I added a couple of vitamin pills for dessert. As I sat eating, enjoying the sound of the river lapping at my feet, I admired the dozen or so dragonflies that were flitting about the small clearing gathering in their evening meal. My admiration stemmed from the fact that their meal was composed largely of mosquitoes.

The evening wore on and the firecrackers—and perhaps a few rifles—began to sound, warming up for the Fourth now only two days away. All the village dogs were going bananas, and to add to the clatter, dozens of hyped-up long-nosed riverboats roared by our point, like raucous motorcycles, gunned ahead on all burners by adolescents of all ages.

The noise began to die down about ten, but I stayed awake until midnight, to take several photos of the sun setting below the tree line of Fort Yukon directly to the *north*! This far north the sun follows a nearly circular course about the sky, dipping

Sunset on the northern horizon at midnight.

below the horizon for only an hour or two each night. I felt that I needed photographic proof to corroborate what my senses were telling me. I had made a similar photographic attempt at Dawson on the day after the year's longest day, gaining a fine midnight sunset in the northern sky. But the effect had been less pronounced there, surrounded as Dawson is by high hills. My photographic efforts complete, I drifted off to sleep with the entire sky over Fort Yukon a deep, almost vibrating red.

I woke about seven or eight the next morning and pushed myself up to take a look outside. To my surprise, I realized that the palm of the hand I was leaning on was very sore. It had in fact been increasing in soreness over the past day or so, but I had only really noticed it just then. It was my right hand, and the soreness seemed to be inside the hand in a line running toward my wrist between my thumb and fingers. I kneaded it for a moment, then forgot about it as I went about my morning chores. I talked with Rich as I puttered about the tent and learned that he intended to go over to the town and do a number of errands: He had stayed in camp the day before, preferring to bake some excellent bannock bread rather than venture into the major metropolis of the Alaskan Yukon on an empty stomach.

Once my morning duties were done—they largely consisted of dumping all my provisions out of my food bag, so that I might find breakfast materials, and then dumping everything back in again—I hopped into the kayak and hurried back up the slough to the Indian Center, because I had been told that the Center had showers for public use. This was to be my first bath since Dawson, and in the already hot Fort Yukon morning I knew that I needed one. But to my anguish (and that of anyone who happened near me?), the Center was closed for the Fourth of July weekend. How awful! I got back into the boat and paddled back down to the other end of the town, where I busied myself with mail and a bit of further shopping. I spent quite a bit of time in the post office, mailing a package of unneeded items home (exposed film, excess film, and an insulated sweatshirt—the day's temperature soared to nearly 100 degrees). I also answered the letters I had received, learning once again that while it is very nice to receive letters from friends while traveling, it can be hell having to answer them all at one sitting—or in this case, standing.

While I was in the post office, I realized that it is surely the center of such a town as Fort Yukon, both its means of communication with and source of goods from the outside world. There was a constant flow of people in and out, talking over the life of the town while getting their mail. One Indian man especially enchanted me, as a paradigm for the modern Yukoner, strangely caught between the past and the future: He complained about the high electric bill he had received, and between them he and the postmaster deduced that it was caused by the man's new micro-wave oven, which he was using to heat sandwiches in his log cabin.

With my duties in Fort Yukon done, I was quite happy to paddle back to camp; Fort Yukon had little of appeal, and its heat and dust made it even less attractive. I was ready to leave, had in fact conducted all my morning's activities with the intention of leaving. But when I got back to camp at about three, I found that Rich had received an invitation to tea for later that afternoon. I asked if he would care to travel through the evening once he got back, but Rich decided that he would rather stay at Fort Yukon a second night. So I said goodbye to Rich, wished him well in his travels on down the river, and watched him paddle off to town. After he left, I relaxed for a few minutes, unwinding from my dash about town and watching the thermometer rise from 89 to 106 degrees when I laid it on the ground in the sun.

I also thought about Rich. With up to a whole day's lead on him, and aware of my slowly mounting desire to pile up miles in order to get off the unending Flats, I had no doubt that I had seen him for the last time on the river. I had traveled no more than half a day away from Rich down nearly 800 miles of the Yukon, yet I realized that I hardly knew him, beyond some of his simpler likes and dislikes and enthusiasms. I knew, for example, that Rich was very particular with all of his equipment, very concerned with its quality, which was excellent throughout. Rich also enjoyed reading Robert Service, he enjoyed good food (his meals were sensible and basic, while mine would have served nicely as trimmings for his), and he possessed a quiet but abiding love for the outdoors and all it held.

Rich also enjoyed being on his own: As is the case with most people who enjoy the wilderness, I believe he found himself perfectly good company. Probably it is this last which caused me not to know Rich very well after being with him for so many days. I think both of us were rather put out at how much we liked having the other person around. We had both set off to go down the Yukon River alone and ended by discovering the usefulness of having another person about: If nothing else, it made one confident that whatever it was that "went bump in the night" would get the other person first and then be too full to make a meal of both of us. In other words, when you are lying alone in your tent, with nobody at all nearby, there is no telling what is lurking about just the other side of those tent walls. With another tent standing next to yours, however, somehow the charmed circle expands and you sleep undisturbed through the night. It's something that I didn't know before this trip, but while one person is alone, two makes a crowd, and man—at least this man—evidently sleeps better in the midst of such a crowd. In any case, while we both wanted to act as though we were traveling completely alone, time and again—as you have seen—we just happened to find ourselves making camp alongside the other. I feel we gained a good deal from traveling together as we did, but I know we also lost much of that elusive element of "lonely adventure" which we both were seeking. As a result, we were surprisingly uncommunicative about our experiences even as we lived them. And, too, it is amazing how quickly "Oh, look at that incredible cloud" and similar observations about one's natural surroundings begin to wear.

In the final analysis, Rich seemed a quiet and gentle person committed to the principle of doing rather than talking. As a result of watching him in action, I knew that Rich was very adept at handling his large, heavy canoe, that he was quite at home in wild settings, and that he was an enjoyable traveling companion. Even as I sat across from Fort Yukon, watching him paddling to town, I felt sorry that I had not known him better.

Six months later, I was to receive a letter from Rich explaining that he had been as exhausted by his last days in the Flats as I was to become, and had ended his "Yukon Summer" at Ruby, the next village beyond Tanana. In the letter, he had this to say about his uncompleted trip to the Bering Sea:

> It concerned me for some time that I did not finish what I had started, though it seemed very prudent, at the time, to stop and return here to Skagway. This concern has mostly passed, not because of any real rational progression of ideas but merely the passing of time. It seems likely that someday I will go back and finish the river from Ruby to the sea, but when is not important. Knowing that I will return is some solace in itself.

The temperature dropped almost instantly once I got out onto the flowing water. The current carried me in a sweeping curve past the town and around to the right of an island that fronts it, then away out of sight. I managed to keep track of where I was for perhaps a mile, then settled back in surrender to the current's random course, unable to make any match between the islands I could see around me and the shapes representing islands on my topo map. I paddled a good deal as I went, releasing the pent-up energy acquired during my brief stay in Fort Yukon. Six hours of paddling, in combination with the fast current, took me almost 45 miles beyond Fort Yukon that afternoon and evening.

By the time I stopped, the fleecy white clouds on the horizon had become a great platform of black supported by dark sheets of rain pouring down in the distance on each side of me but never quite reaching the environs of the river. I pulled the boat up on a very attractive slice of sandy beach running along the river's channel on the upper end of a small island. In contrast with Fort Yukon, it was very peaceful and quiet on this little island, and even the hordes of mosquitoes batting against my headnet couldn't upset the evening.

I made a small fire just outside my tent and had an excellent meal of soup, crackers and Postum. There were finally a few drops of rain, but not enough to mar the evening, nor to cut down on the masses of mosquitoes. I made some attempt to figure out where I might be on the river, using my map and compass and sighting on a far-off rounded dome I happened to spot low on the horizon between a gap in the trees downriver. After this fruitless but entertaining effort, I anchored the boat to shore with uncommon care—feeling very alone without Rich's presence or proximity—and went to sleep with the drone of hungry mosquitoes all about my lonely tent.

17   Another Short Chapter: Mosquitoes

I feel compelled to devote at least a few short pages to a subject which is inescapable—literally inescapable—for anyone traveling on the Yukon during the summer: the infernal beast scientifically labeled Culcidae, but often given rather more colorful names by those who must suffer the blood-sucking attentions of this horrid family of insects. While I was unable to verify sworn testimony that these vermin have been known to seize and fly off with whole bears and moose, it certainly does not seem unlikely. As truthful an observer as Jack London has testified that he once saw two mosquitoes pull apart the strands of his mosquito netting to let a third thirsty member of their party through, and at another time he swears that he encountered the most fearsome variety of this beast, that with blood-sucking equipment at both ends.

One begins to get a slightly anemic feeling under the ministrations of these undersized ambulatory blood-bottles whom I can only characterize as nefarious, pernicious, incidious, malicious and dastardly, also ever-present. Mosquitoes are driven away by rain? That's a myth, at least in the Yukon. They won't come out in the hot sun? Another myth. The wind drives them away? Ha! With only one human body per billion mosquitoes, they must work full time to satisfy everyone's appetite for blood.

It is surprising how easily the incessant attention of mosquitoes can drive an otherwise reasonably sane person batty, even when that person is protected by the finest repellents, head-nets and mosquito-proof tents that money can buy. (Repellent, unfortunately, seems to have a half-life of about 20 minutes.) The damned things are always *there*, just beyond your netting, waiting to get at you. And when there are enough of them about your tent at night—like perhaps the one or two thousand that I believe ringed my tent at times on the river—they make an uncanny high-pitched whine all about you, like miniature band-saws warming up to cut you into shreds.

Under the impact of this seige, you find yourself doing very odd things. I was often guilty of loudly cheering dragonflies, numerous on the river, as they flitted about gathering in their evening meal of mosquitoes. What could possibly be a more just fate for a mosquito than to be suddenly seized and chomped by the gorgon-head a dragonfly must seem to them? I even wondered if it might not be possible to train great packs of dragonflies, so that they might circle a person constantly, eating the mosquitoes by the bushel before they could eat you. I cheered not only dragonflies, but also swallows (which nest here and there in clay banks by the river) and anything else that looked like it might eat the iniqui-tous creatures. *Anything* that kills mosquitoes *has* to be good.

Rich reacted much the same way. He is a very nice fellow, very gentle, a person who would not want to hurt a single living creature in the world. Except mosquitoes! He spent what must have amounted to hours trying to pull them by their probosci through the weave of his tent's mosquito netting.

But the battle was not entirely one sided. No matter how fast I managed to enter my tent through the zippered mosquito screen, there were sure to be dozens of mosquitoes in with me. Unable to escape, each of them was carefully hunted down and dispatched before I attempted to go to sleep. I must admit to experiencing a certain glee with this chore, as the feeling swept over me that it was now *my* turn to harass the little ever-present monsters. I found that I preferred the personal "thumb-touch" method for those I found in the tent, placing my thumb on the beasts as they rested against the tent fabric, then churning it around just enough to scramble them to death. I reserved the "blast-em-flat" technique for those I discovered actually sucking up my vital juices. This last method was needed only a few hundred times a day, as, luckily, the mosquitoes tended to be few out on the river itself.

It isn't that the Yukon mosquitoes are an impossible obstacle to the traveler. They aren't. (Although I shudder to think what they would be like for a person traveling without a headnet or tent for protection on shore.) But I would have dearly loved to travel in shorts rather than long jeans, especially in the heat of the Flats and beyond, and I also felt myself badly in need of frequent swims in the river. Yet neither of these were possible in the face of the hordes of mosquitoes brought to buzzing life by the summer sun. If there could only be some way to line all of Culcidae up and shoot them once and for all, I'm sure many people in the Yukon would sell their much-bitten souls to the devil for the right to pull the trigger.

18   The Flats, Part III: Beaver and Stevens Village

I woke about nine on the Fourth of July, dressed in boots and rain parka and headnet in order to break through the gauntlet of mosquitoes ringing my tent, and I made my escape to open water by ten. I paddled for the next six hours, threading my way through the endless islands, pausing now and then to get the direction of the current, then hurrying along it. Surprisingly, I actually knew where I was on the maps when I approached Beaver, a small Indian settlement on the right side of the river 60 miles from my morning start.

On my approach to the town I was curious about how deserted it seemed. I beached the boat at the foot of a road-like cut in the bank that led up to the dirt street running between the river and a row of log cabins. Straightening up from the boat, I heard a noise and turned to see an Indian man standing at the top of the inclined cut, looking down at me. He was dressed in a patched coat several sizes too large, and his pants were so wide that they flapped about his legs. He said nothing, and his face didn't change its expression when I waved up to him and said hello; then he abruptly began to run stiff-legged down the cut. As he came silently down on me, I wondered if I was about to be attacked. But he stopped only a foot or so from me and began to speak excitedly.

I couldn't make out a word the man was saying, but the problem involved more than the man's halting English. He also seemed to have some sort of speech defect that forced him to slur and mangle his words. He kept pointing up to the village and I thought he was asking me something, but I simply didn't know what to do. I finally smiled and tried to calm him, then went about my business of getting the boat up onto shore and changing from my tennis shoes to rubber boots to gain some further protection against the mosquitoes swarming about.

With everything secure, I walked up the cut with my strange welcoming committee close behind. I never did find out what the man was trying to say. When we got to the line of cabins, I asked about the village store and he led me to a larger building. Then, when I went up to read a note on the door ("Closed for Fourth of July Picnic, Everyone Attend") he disappeared. I heard some voices sounding faintly from behind the store, so I walked back to a cabin just behind, to ask where the post office might be and why the town was so empty. I stuck my head into the cabin and found four people—two Indian women moving about the single large room, and two men, one white, one Indian, stretched out on two large beds in the middle of the room. They looked up, asked me to come in, and the Indian man on the bed explained that most of the town was out at a Fourth of July picnic in a meadow back behind the town. He also said that the post office was further down the main street, in a private house hidden in the trees. I asked what sort of a town Beaver had been originally, and the Indian answered that it had been a gold-rush town. Then he invited me to come in and pull up a chair.

And damn if I didn't do a Coffee Creek all over again. "Oh, no, no thank you, thanks very much" came out before I could think, and I was back outside. I wanted to sit down in a cabin with the people of such a village as Beaver; yet here again, through some sort of reflex, I refused just such an invitation. And there wasn't another chance; one thing that I was to realize on this trip is that up in the north the people ask you only once, not the three or four times that is socially common and expected in the lower states. Courtesy here involves letting each person go his own way, without pressuring him in your own direction. If an invitation is refused once, it isn't forced on a person again.

I kicked myself down the street to the band of trees hiding a small barn and a neat log cabin. A young Indian man was working over a motor in the barn. I approached him and asked if he was the post office. "Try my wife inside," he answered pleasantly, then went back to work. I stepped to the door of the cabin, knocked, then leaned inside and called. The inside of the house was a surprise, looking like any inexpensive but well-furnished apartment or suburban house in the states and giving no hint from the inside of its log exterior or the rugged temperatures it must withstand each winter. It had several rooms, and the woman of the household came bustling out from one of the back ones, apologizing for the "messiness" of the house and explaining that she was trying to get her husband and her son ready for a trip. The house looked absolutely neat and spotless to my eyes, but I guess women have to say that phrase no matter where they are.

I asked about mail—a friend had threatened to mail a letter to every post office on the river, and almost succeeded—and she immediately disappeared into the town's post office, a small cubical built into the corner of the cabin. After a good deal of rummaging about, she came up with a post card for me. I asked what life was like for a resident of Beaver. She said that she liked Beaver better than a bigger city, took no notice of the harsh winters, and enjoyed fishing during the summer while her husband worked at fire fighting. During the winter he brought in needed money by trapping. We talked for a few more minutes, then I thanked the woman and her husband, who was now standing at the door.

"How far have you come?" he asked.

"From Bennett Lake."

"Oh, yeah? How do you find the mosquitoes?"

"Oh, not too bad out on the water, although five of them got me on the ankle just when I landed."

"Yeah, they're the worst this year that we've ever seen."

"Really? I'm glad to hear that; that its not just because I'm a newcomer on the river."

"Oh, yes, they bite Indians, too."

I'm not sure—the man's delivery was very dry—but this last seemed vaguely like a zinger, a put down. I laughed anyway—rather awkwardly—and made my departure. I suspect that there is an understandable resentment among Indians (and Eskimos) toward whites in Alaska, and it is also reasonable to assume that the natives along the Yukon might feel some resentment against travelers such as myself wandering through their villages and snapping pictures of their "quaint" homes and "amusing" belongings. I certainly did not have such feelings—in fact I was in awe of how well they have adapted to the brutally diverse living conditions the Yukon region forces upon them—but I could see how they might misunderstand an outsider's interest in their lifestyle.

I walked back up the dusty road fronting the river. Nobody seemed to be moving about the town, and I was undisturbed as I sat on an oil drum at the top of the cut, wondering about the town, about communication with people, about how hard it is to really know what people mean when they talk with you. Then I said the hell with it, went back down the cut in the bank, got back into the kayak and, with a sense of relief at returning to my simpler world of flowing water and a beautiful cloud-spattered sky, paddled back out into the river's current.

The river curves to the left beyond Beaver and, a few miles down from the small town, I found a perfect spot for dinner on a sandbar to the right of the river. I pulled the boat to shore, carried my things up to a large log half-buried in the sand, and made a small cooking fire from driftwood bits. As I ate, I enjoyed watching the sun, with its evening tint of gold, stretching long shadows across the sand to the river. I finished my dinner and noticed for the first time that for some reason no mosquitoes were around. Taking advantage of this fantastic opportunity, I spent a long time washing in the river, which was brisk but not agonizingly cold, and a nice contrast to the hot muggy air of the Flats.

Since it was the Fourth of July, I set off several firecrackers from a pack I had acquired in Fort Yukon. I was amazed at how quiet they seemed as they exploded right beside me, and how roaringly loud they were echoing back from the islands across the river. It was fun to join the Alaskans in this revelry—I could hear similar reports drifting down from Beaver—but after six or eight of the blasts I realized I really preferred the normal quiet of the river.

At about eight I finished washing up the dinner dishes and myself, repacked the kayak, then slipped back into its cockpit and returned to the river. It was quite wide here, and I thought that I could see the main current burbling around some fallen trees on the far left side of the channel. The current seemed to continue rippling down the left side of the channel for a mile or so, to a point where the channel made a right turn out of sight. On the other hand, a fairly swift current also seemed to be flowing along right in front of the sandbar where I had dinner. But it turned to the right of a small island at the end of the bar and appeared to head directly for the right bank of the river. I puzzled over these two alternatives and finally decided to go with the current nearest me. It seemed to know what it was doing, and in any case it had me fairly in its grip, making escape to the other side and the alternate current a difficult if not impossible task.

The flow of water carried me along the sharp right bend around the end of the sandbar and then hustled me toward the right-hand shore. Drifting logs and other debris seemed to be going in the same direction with me, so when I spotted a break in the right shore through which the current seemed to be pouring, I paddled toward it and passed through to a narrower channel.

I truly have no idea where I traveled that evening. The map, which had kept me accurately informed of my location for a mile or two leading up to Beaver, and again from Beaver down to my dinner stop at the sandbar, showed no evidence of the network of channels, of the twists and turns and curves of the river, that I now found myself working along. The current had decreased once I passed through the cut in the bank, and it continued to diminish as I moved further and further into the maze of small islands and rambling waterways. As the night wore on I began to worry that I had allowed myself to wander into a slough that led nowhere. My course certainly was not on the map.

But there was nothing to do about it except continue, so I kept paddling as the deep blue sky overhead grew darker and darker under banks of towering black clouds. I pushed on for three hours, looking for any sort of a place to stop for the night but finding none that would do. The islands were all thickly cloaked with brush extending right down into the water. Finally, I spotted a narrow strip of flat, fern-covered sandy bank running like a little ledge between the river and the dense shrubbery of an island. I beached the boat and was met by a cloud of tiny but voracious mosquitoes rising from the green ferns. I got the tent up just in time not only to avoid being eaten alive but also to escape the heavy rain that abruptly began to fall.

Inside the tent I looked over the map again but could find no clues as to where I might be. According to the map, I had spent the last three hours paddling over solid land, or at least as solid as land can get in the Flats. Yet there was not only water but a still-discernible current running along the channel just outside the tent, so I could only assume that it would lead me somewhere the next day.

I felt quite tired as I lay inside the tent, really very tired. And depressed. I had a new blister on my left hand from all the paddling through the evening's slow current, my muscles felt strained and "snapless," and my right hand, which had felt sore in Fort Yukon, was now worse and seemed almost sprained. I kneaded the sensitive palm for a few minutes, then tuned out the abrasive buzzing of the mosquitoes clustered about the netting at the tent entrance and fell asleep.

The next day was not much of an improvement in terms of traveling or mosquitoes or my fading spirits and energy. I woke in the morning almost more tired than I had felt the night before, and by the time I had packed up and burst out through the ambuscade the mosquitoes had arranged during the night, I was ready for another rest instead of the ten hours of hacking and cutting at the virtually still waters which lay ahead.

I felt very tired all day, and I was exasperated at how poorly I was traveling and how much my hand was beginning to ache. During one pause in my futile efforts to get a successful stroke going, I looked carefully at several of the maps and realized one of the problems I was facing. From Bennett Lake to Dawson, the drop in altitude is about 1,100 feet over 550 miles; from Dawson to Fort Yukon, the drop is roughly 600 feet in 460 miles. But from Beaver to the Bering Sea, a little over 1,000 miles, the river drops only another 362 feet. Obviously, the current would be slowing down. In terms of my present position, this information reassured me that I was probably not lost or on the wrong channel after all. But I did wonder for the first time just how far I was going to be able to hack my way down this river with only the present languorous current behind me.

It rained a little in the morning as I struggled along the sluggish and meandering river, but then the clouds drifted away and the sun came blazing down to lift my spirits a little. I paddled with more vigor and, by late afternoon, had reached an encouragingly wider channel that was less clogged with islands. Then I began once again to be able to spot where I was by comparing the topo maps to my surroundings. I had apparently taken the right course, for I seemed to be nearing Stevens Village, my next destination on the Yukon after Beaver.

I finally paddled down a cut between two islands choked with floating debris, made a right turn, and found myself facing Stevens Village down a long narrow approach between the shore and a strip of island on the left. I wearily paddled toward the town and at about six o'clock slipped the kayak in beside several other boats against a sloping bank that fronted the village.

Stevens Village, unlike Beaver, had a large number of people moving about when I reached shore. One young man carrying a five-gallon can strode down the bank, walked out over the moored boats, and scooped the muddy river into his can. He nodded and smiled hello when I said "Hi," as though people climbing out of tiny kayaks were a normal daily occurrence. He told me where I could find the store, then carried the heavy tin up the slope and into a cabin. A group of kids, their new and fashionable clothing quite out of keeping with the dirt road and log cabins fronting the river, were milling about, displaying no signs of interest in me beyond asking if I had any matches to spare; they had run out of matches but not Fourth of July firecrackers.

I walked down to the store—a tiny cabin with shelves set into two walls and a partition dividing the shop from the living quarters —and as an almost ritual act purchased some candy bars and a can of soft drink from the proprietor, a busy Indian woman who muttered to herself about the day's business as she waited on me. Then I returned to the Quisnam to find three Indian boys sitting beside it, touching the canvas deck now and then and obviously wishing that they could get into it and give it a try. I sat down with them and drank my soft drink while answering their questions and asking a few of my own.

Two of them—Marty and Tom—seemed to be about 12, while Herman may have been a couple of years younger. They wore jeans and boots and pullover shirts, and each of them had the same thick, straight, jet-black hair worn in a Prince Valiant or bowl-cut style around their full coppery-brown faces. Marty, the most talkative of the three and evidently their leader, informed me that he went to school in Fairbanks but that he was begging his parents to let him stay in Stevens Village during the winters. "Winter is fun," he said, "because you get to use the snow-sleds and dog teams and go out trapping." All three were eager to spot themselves on my topo map and to show me all the points of interest on it. Marty located his father's fishing camp down the river and insisted that I stop there and say hello to his father for him.

We sat there for about half an hour talking about this and that and passing around a squirming, white-haired little bundle of husky pup that Tom "liberated" from its mother, part of a team of dogs staked out just beside the river. Then the boys led me to the post office, located at the upper end of town. It was already closed for the night, but two old Indian men, standing in front of a nearby cabin and surveying the course of the evening, told me in rough-hewn English that the post office would open in the morning and that if I wanted to stay for the night, I really ought to make camp somewhere down the river, away from town. "These kids, all they do is make noise all night," one grinned up at me, shaking his head. "There's no way anyone can sleep when the summer sun is up."

After saying goodbye to my young friends, I took the advice of their elders and moved my boat downriver. The banks I found below the town were nearly vertical and almost 10 feet high, and I began to wonder if I shouldn't just forget about checking for mail and proceed further downriver to find a better campsite. But it had been a long day and I knew perfectly well that I had no guarantee that I would find a better campsite further along, so I pulled the boat up against the bank below the town's airstrip, tying it up in a suspiciously odorous little backwash. It took a bit of scrambling to get my things out of the boat and up the crumbling bank, but I managed it and made camp to one side of the grass airstrip.

It was very hot with the sun bright and low over the water, the air muggy and close, so I rigged up a tarp-and-stick shade

Herman, Marty and Tom at Stevens Village.

beside the tent, then cooked a dinner of macaroni and cheese and ate it inside the tent, away from the—you guessed it—mosquitoes. The evening began to cool as I ate, and I looked forward to a good, comfortable sleep. As I sat there, eating and thinking, I realized that Stevens Village marked roughly 1,000 miles of travel for me down the Yukon from Bennett Lake. I also realized that I seemed to be getting more and more tired as day followed long hot day on the Flats. I would reach my goal of Tanana, that was certain. But whether I could continue on from there, I didn't know. I was very tired.

19   From Bad to Good: The Longest Day

The heat of the sun forced me out of the tent and into action at eight the next morning. It was already hot outside as well, making the process of breaking camp rather unpleasant in the bundle of clothing I was wearing as a defense against the mosquitoes. When everything was packed away in the boat, I walked back along a path running through the forest and reached the town just as it was coming awake. The first person I passed was a sleepy man starting an outdoor stove for his morning breakfast. Then I nodded to three Indian women seated on a bench in the shade of one of the log cabins by the road. They seemed to be there for a quiet morning's talk, enjoying the river and the early morning peace. They all nodded back, smiling among themselves and even including me in their amusement at my appearance: scuffed and muddy boots, dirty jeans, a shrunken, badly soiled sweatshirt, and my unkempt beard and hair.

The post office was still closed, but an Indian man pointed off to the postmaster's cabin which was set well back from the homes fronting the river. I walked back to it, knocked, and was met by a man pulling on his pants. When I asked if the postmaster were about, he said that indeed he was, but that he would not be opening the post office until he got his pants on and had some breakfast. It seemed a reasonable answer, so I walked back to the store to wait, drinking Orange Crushes and talking with the store owner, Lillian Petka.

Lillian Petka struck me as, if not a typical example, at least a remarkable instance of the many Indian people who find themselves somewhat at odds with both their old culture and the white man's new one. On the one hand, her English was not terribly clear, sounding just the way anyone might trying to speak a second language, and her store forced one to wonder if she had ever seen a "real" store. She also talked with particular enthusiasm and pride about going out to the Indian fishing camps during the summer and about the unearthly cold that she and her friends casually endure through the winter. On the other hand, just outside of Lillian's small log cabin store, there was a strange contraption, a gigantic tilted dish which looked as though it were made out of scrap iron rods. In fact, this dish was a powerful radio transmitter with which Lillian maintains radio contact for the village with the outside world. Via a satellite floating somewhere over New Mexico, Lillian broadcasts medical reports each day from her village to the district hospital in Tanana and receives instructions from the doctors there for the care of minor ailments. (A plane comes from the hospital for more serious emergencies.) Lillian is as conversant with satellite communications as I might be with my telephone; and because of that satellite, she and many other Alaskan natives were hearing reports from the astronauts walking the moon before the average American ever saw and heard them on television. Thus, Lillian not only stretches from her Indian past to my white man's present, but on into the scientist's fantastic future. And she does it with as much calm and serenity as she shows in selling me another can of Orange Crush.

It was a quiet morning in Lillian's store, the sun lighting and warming its interior, and we sat talking about this and that for some time, she sitting behind the table that served as desk and sales counter while I occupied an old upholstered chair next to an oil can by the door. When it was finally time for the post office to open, I thanked Lillian for the morning's conversation and walked along the sunlit street toward the other end of the village. The three women were still sitting in front of the cabin where I had passed them earlier. They looked up and laughed to find me tromping past again, and one of them, a rolly-polly woman, grinned hugely and asked "Haven't we seen you somewhere before?"

"Well," I answered, "I could be twins, you know."

"Yes, of course, that must be it."

Inane conversation, but produced out of a real feeling of warmth from these women who watched a strange white man clumping up and down their village street in its awakening hours and saw fit to smile and joke with him.

The postmaster had just opened the small post office and attached store, with the assistance of a four-year-old child who watched our transactions with huge eyes. There was no mail for me, despite my friend's assurances, so I walked out between the neat log planter boxes and the extensive vegetable garden at the front entrance of the post office and ambled slowly through the quiet town for the last time. As I passed the three ladies again, I said good-bye and assured them that this would be my last promenade by them. The heavy one wished me a good trip, the others chuckled, and I walked on back to the airfield and my waiting kayak.

The channel running in front of Stevens Village is not the main channel of the river but a slow-moving backwater cut off from the rest of the river by several overlapping, three to four mile long islands. The water veers to the left after passing in front of the town, joining the main river and sliding through a gap in the Fort Hamlin Hills, which form the start of canyon country and the end of the seemingly interminable Flats. It was very hot in the sun on the water as I paddled away from the village. And with almost no current to help me, I found myself already tired, my hand quite sore, and once again had difficulty in establishing a decent stroking rhythm. At last, in desperation, I finally agreed with myself that I would produce 1,000 strokes before I stopped again. Five hundred of these—I forget what rationalization allowed me to stop halfway through—carried me clear of the islands lying in front of Stevens Village and back to the main channel, where the current began to pick up.

My map indicated that a stream might be found near the site of Fort Hamlin, so in the hope of finding some fresh water after the wretched stuff I'd had to drink from the river the day before, I crossed over to the opposite, left-hand side of the river and let the current carry me forward toward the fort and the green-walled canyons beyond. The fort proved to be a couple of log cabins crumbling into the ground, set back and separated from the river by a field of the low ferns and a screen of trees. I found no water there—could hardly look for water—because I aroused a great cloud of mosquitoes that seemed to rise up out of the ferns. They drove me back out onto the river, and it was a good 20 minutes of heavy paddling before I had left the hungry swarms behind.

I was hotter and thirstier than ever as I proceeded along between the canyon walls, hoping to spot another clear, cool freshet pouring down one of the canyon's rocky slopes. It was good to be back between the green canyon walls after five days on the Flats, but the heat and my thirst conspired to prevent my fully enjoying my new surroundings. Finally, I stopped by the mouth of a stream identified as the Waldron on the map, but it proved to be another still-water slough fed by a stream some unknown distance back from the water's edge. Nevertheless I beached the boat, thinking that I would walk back up the side of the slough, find the running stream and get my water.

As usual, I was wearing my camera about my neck, ready to photograph whatever curiosities might rise from the depths or descend from the skies. As I stood up out of the boat I once

The post office in Stevens Village.

again artfully managed to nick another lens cap into the water just an inch or so from the pebbly mud of the steep shore. Of course, it was gone; the shore shelved straight down as soon as it met the water there, and another expensive lens cap was now lying invisibly somewhere just beyond my reach.

Tired, thirsty, now suddenly angry as well, I gave up on the lens cap and scrambled up the wooded hillside beside the slough, determined to find water to pay for the loss of the cap. But from the height of the low hill I could see that the slough continued back for several hundred feet, stagnant and still, and that I would be getting no potable water here. At the same time as I discovered this, the mosquitoes discovered me again and drove me flying down the hillside, where I slipped and banged myself on several tree trunks. Damnable mosquitoes!

Suddenly I ran out of good humor to temper my angry and exhausted condition, and my mood slid to an evil, depressing low. For the first time I was not only tired of body, but of much that surrounded me as well—tired of mosquitoes, tired of being dirty, tired of not being able to drink clean water, tired of hacking away uselessly at paddling, tired of my painful hand, tired of losing things. As I thrashed along in the kayak, trying to get clear of the mosquitoes that still harrassed me, I began to wonder if perhaps 30 days of doing *anything* might not be enough, and if a thousand miles down the fifth largest river in America might not be more than enough.

I even wondered what in the world I thought I was doing on this river at all, and what I had hoped to gain from such a trip. I could not decide in my mind if I were merely tired from the major physical effort of getting through the Flats, or if I were simply unequal to the task I had set for myself. Where I had been able to maintain a steady stroke for five hours and more on Bennett and LaBerge, now I could hardly keep one going for five minutes. It all rather disgusted me. (I was relieved to learn that the journey through the Flats and beyond had wreaked the same sort of punishment on Rich: He was to show up in Tanana as exhausted and tired as I.)

Well, I finally decided, the hell with it, the hell with it all—with the mosquitoes and the river and trying to get anywhere and everything else. I threw the paddle down across the cockpit with an air of finality, got out my book of Thoreau, unsnapped the spray cover, drew my knees up, and settled back to read for the next hour or day or century.

And strangely enough, or perhaps not so strangely, since there often seems to be a balance in such things, out of my black mood grew the best day I spent on the entire trip down the Yukon. I finally found just the sort of clear bubbling little stream that I had hoped for, cascading down a rock wall into the Yukon; and then I continued downriver for a total of 14 hours of travel, during which I traveled almost 90 miles. Of more importance, however, was what happened to my mind during that time; the way it calmed down and then began to expand into the country I was traveling through. By the late evening I reached a state I can only describe as mystical and euphoric, in which I felt that the sun and river and the country all about were working together for my enjoyment, my enlightenment even, and that in some way I was there for their enjoyment as well. Perhaps these feelings were partly the result of reading Thoreau in the outdoor setting, but the ultimate source doesn't seem very important. The experience was very special for me, more than ample recompense and reward in that one evening for all the effort of the trip.

The wonder of this strange evening, arising out of my calmer mood and my reading material and the slant of the sun and perhaps even the arrangement of the stars, was that a long-lost sensory experience returned for my pleasure. For many years I have been aware, as I have aged, of a diminishing ability to receive and appreciate the messages my senses bring to me from the world around me. When I was young, I know that I was able to smell the sunlight hitting the trees and dusty ground, sense its changes, hear living things growing all about me, and respond to the wind as it moved against my skin. But since then, no matter how hard I have tried, I've never been fully able to recapture those abilities. It is as though the daily wear and tear of existence creates layers of scar tissue about the senses, about the soul if you will, blocking the sensations that would make us one with the world. I often thought that this might just be something peculiar to me alone, but then I happened to read what Wordsworth has to say, in the first stanza of his ode "Intimations of Immortality from Recollections of Early Childhood":

> There was a time when meadow, grove, and stream,
> The earth, and every common sight,
>   To me did seem
>   Apparelled in celestial light,
> The glory and the freshness of a dream.
> It is not now as it hath been of yore;—
>   Turn whereso'er I may,
>   By night or day,
> The things which I have seen I now can see no more.

He goes on to say:

> But yet I know, where'er I go,
> That there hath past away a glory from the earth.

As soon as I put down the paddle, as soon as I stopped trying to drive myself through the water, goaded to reach the next destination and the next, I re-discovered the river and the speeding current, which was given to me by the river for nothing, like a gift of friendship. I was actually making very good time down the canyon country, with few demands upon my tired body and sore hand. As the afternoon passed, I became more and more relaxed, far less aware of time and how much of it had to pass before I could round a bend or curve in the river ahead. And as time dilated around me, I realized that I was slowly regaining much of my vanished ability to truly sense my surroundings. It was sheer pleasure to simply sit and look at the texture of the canyon walls, and the patterns of the trees and shrubs growing on them, as they slid by.

The river, once it entered the canyon lands below the Flats, completely changed its character. As if eager to re-define itself clearly after so much aimless meandering, the river became narrow—perhaps a half mile wide—and swift, with curiously few of the whirls and boils that marked the current on its upper reaches. Perhaps the gorge here was very deep, and the water flows smoothly, unimpeded by any obstacles on the bottom. I could tell that I was moving rapidly by watching the shores slip by, but it was difficult to feel the speed of the water due to its smooth surface. The river was also strikingly empty of islands.

The river took on the form of a prodigious, slightly squiggly S-curve on its way to Rampart; and at about six, having completed the top curve of the S, I tried to stop on the first major island I came to, Kalka, to prepare something to eat. I could see no place where I might stop, however, and by simply coming near the island I stirred up great hordes of mosquitoes. I was in a far better mood now than earlier in the day, so I simply laughed at them and sped on my way. I was content to go without a formal supper, as I had food stashed about the cockpit of the boat to nibble; and by floating on I allowed the magic of the evening to build and work upon me.

On Crescent Island, just down the straightaway from Kalka, a family of crows or huge ravens was squabbling loudly at the tops of a stand of spruce trees. They sounded like mad women testing their screams out on each other, but their noise only emphasized the great peace on all sides. I kept watch on these raucous birds as I drifted by, even turning the boat so that I could look at them head-on, then I returned to Thoreau. I was reading *Walden*, and I was in the chapter called "Solitude":

> I find it wholesome to be alone the greater part of the time.
> To be in company, even with the best, is soon wearisome and
> dissipating. I love to be alone, I never found the companion
> that was so companionable as solitude.

I also found it wholesome to be alone this evening, drifting down the Yukon without another human anywhere nearby. In fact, I realized that I had never really felt alone—despite being away from other people—during any part of the journey. I had so much company here: that duck that just landed nearby; the ouzels flitting along the shore with their strangely down-turned wings when I happened near; the flights of geese and ducks with their intricately shifting patterns overhead; each bend of the river; every tree on shore; the endless play of never-setting sunlight on the clouds floating overhead; the rocks bulking up the canyon wall and here combining with a sheaf of fallen trees to form a pagan monument

Reflections in the river.

alive with ancient unknown powers; the sound of the breeze, and the water hissing over a root or stubborn rock on shore. Everything demanded and returned my attention that evening. The effect of constantly changing, subtly changing vistas was almost hypnotic, the warm sun adding to the effect.

Finally, as though wishing to underscore the sensations pouring into me from all sides, a wind which I could not feel ran gently along the line of poplars standing as a border to the shore. It turned the leaves of the trees, switching the green outer surface for the silvery underside, creating a wave of silver light that flowed slowly through the trees for a mile down the shore. Everything was so calm and quiet that the tiniest motion of the boat brought intricate patterns to the still river surface. It was one of the most beautiful, unforgettable moments I have ever experienced, the culmination of a perfect evening. Hours later, almost 90 miles from Stevens Village, I pulled the boat to shore.

20 Rampart, Tanana, and the
End of a Journey

"Begin at the beginning," the King said, very gravely, "and go on till you come to the end: then stop." (Lewis Carroll, *Alice in Wonderland*)

One of the pleasures in traveling down a river, or taking any sort of voyage or slow journey, involves the sense of progress and achievement in starting at some point and continuing until you reach another point, where you will stop. When you have stopped, you can look back in your mind, or on the surface of a map, and actually review the distance you have covered, the experiences you have acquired. So much of life today involves formless activity without any real beginning or end—aimless pushings-about of paper and people and money—that it is often a real relief to engage in an activity with a definite start and finish. Of course, even on a voyage, it may sometimes be difficult to determine where the end should come.

After the "longest day," I spent two more days traveling on the Yukon, going from my campsite just above Rampart to Tanana, 80 miles away. For most of those 80 miles, my mind was occupied with a debate over whether I should end my journey at Tanana or continue on down the river. My tiredness, my sore hand, my inability to develop a really good stroking rhythm were all still with me, and they all suggested that I ought to stop. In addition, there was the consideration that flying from Tanana to Fairbanks, where I was eventually to catch a jet for home, was by far the cheapest route by which to leave the river. On the other side of the coin there stood the weighty argument that this was a "chance of a lifetime" and that I ought to seize it and continue as far down the river as possible. Inevitably, however, the other side of my mind would answer "Perhaps Tanana *is* as far as possible." In any case, the battle raged on as I alternately drifted or tried to paddle my way along.

The penultimate day of my journey, July 7, began about eight, with the sun once again heating the inside of my tent beyond endurance and forcing me up after a scant six hours of sleep. Once outside I discovered myself to be in another of those rare "king's X" zones of protection against the mosquitoes, and instantly, a

Rampart.

great orgy of washing—of clothes and body and boat—took place.
As I worked over the Quisnam I was amazed at how much punishment the kayak had absorbed with no visible damage. It had been
beached roughly innumerable times, had run aground too many
times for comfort, and had served, seemingly years ago, as an
icebreaker on Bennett. Yet the kayak still looked fresh and almost
new, certainly ready for any number of additional miles down
the river.

The "life-support systems" were also in remarkably good shape
and—excepting that bloody stove—were all functioning well. In
fact, the only weak-link of the whole set-up seemed to be the
captain of the craft. But I couldn't ignore how tired I felt, nor
how sore my hand was. (Later, in Tanana, a doctor told me that
the problem was merely a strain, and that such pain is very common
among any workers, such as plumbers, who do a lot of rotating
motions with their hands. I was of course rotating my right hand
at the wrist every time I took a paddle stroke on the left side
of the boat.)

I reached the little town of Rampart, backed by high hills and
thick forest on the left shore of the river, before the town had
really awakened for the day. As I beached the boat and walked

up to the main road running along the river, there were only some sleepy dogs and a few children to take notice. I walked to the largest structure on the road—a two-story building of sun-bleached wood that proclaimed itself to be the "Weisner Trading Co."—and found three men inside, comfortably arranged around the proverbial pot-bellied stove of the north, enjoying the process of slowly waking to the new day. One of the men was stupendously fat, and I believe he was Ira Weisner, the owner of the store. (My confusion on this comes from his talking about "Weisner" in the third person, but his friend called him Ira.)

The inside of the store was a wonderful dusty jumble of ancient goods, boxes and bales of strange items, low ceilings, and a big pool table groaning under further piles of merchandise. I looked it all over, then purchased a can of strawberries for breakfast and sat eating and chatting with the men. At one point Ira told his friend, a man from Fairbanks, to show me the gold that was stashed in the antique cash register. The friend got up, tall and bony, opened the register, and dropped about two pounds of gold into my hand. It was in the form of large, smoothly rounded nuggets that gleamed dully in the light filtering through the dusty windows behind us. As I handled the nuggets, I couldn't help thinking "Did all those men work as incredibly hard as they did for *this*?"

I left Rampart after passing a good deal of the morning sitting inside the store, sitting outside watching the river flow past, or simply wandering about. An hour or two later I was once again battening down the boat, and my mind, because a portion of the river ahead, lined with high canyon walls and squeezed by Senatis Mountain, was identified on the topo maps as simply "The Rapids." These were the rapids of Rampart Canyon, the site where the dam to flood the Flats was to have been constructed. I readied myself for the confrontation and was sorely disappointed to find myself through and beyond "The Rapids" without seeing anything of them. Undoubtedly there is more to them when the river is lower (one man in Rampart had said the river was ten feet higher than normal). I certainly had not wanted another Five Finger Rapids, but I would not have minded a little something to liven up my day.

It was early evening when I stopped for dinner in a ferny meadow backed by the dilapidated remains of what had probably been an Indian fishing camp. Dinner was a slowly eaten, enjoyable affair of rice and sirloin tips out of a can, tea, and the inevitable jello pudding, which for some reason this evening came out roughly the consistency of Elmer's Glue. Everything was cooked over a

Evening shadows from the green banks of the Yukon.

small fire that seemed to help keep the mosquitoes away—an occurrence that went a long ways toward making up for my spoiled dessert. Despite my wash that morning, I still felt grubby and unkempt, even somewhat out of sorts because of this, but the food definitely helped improve my mood. The debate over how far I was going to go down the river had raged all day in my mind, and I was quite tired of the whole matter as a result.

The evening dragged on as I continued down the river, looking for a place to stop for the night. There were few possibilities due to the high water and the thick brush that grew right down the banks, but I finally found a likely spot, a low sandbar rising beside the edge of Sixteen Mile Island, so named because it lies 16 miles above Tanana.

The mosquitoes must have called a convention on Sixteen Mile Island especially for my arrival, because there were thousands of them. These were a smaller edition of the usual Yukon monster, but they amply made up in numbers what they lacked in size. Swatting and cursing, I beached the boat, threw my ensolite pad, the map case, my water bottles, the food bag and the sleeping bag and pads up on the shore as quickly as I could. Then out came the rudder pedals and the clothing bag, and only at that point could I get at the tent which was my shelter and protection against the blood-thirsty hordes.

I shook out the tent from its bag, spread it out on the ground and pegged down its sides as quickly as possible. Then in went the inverted Vs of the support poles at each end, and I completed its raising with a complicated dance about its edges, pulling lines taut and pegging them down in the soft sand. It only took a few more moments to zip open the tent's mosquito screen, throw everything inside and leap in after, and then I could finally take off my headnet and begin the satisfying process of killing off the 40 or 50 mosquitoes who had the temerity to follow me through the netting. Having finished this, I could lie back at last and contemplate the humming mass of mosquitoes clustered about the front of the tent, hoping for my return.

Each evening on the river since just below LaBerge had more or less followed the same script as this, but never with quite these numbers of mosquitoes. Sixteen Mile Island was truly the record-holder in terms of mosquitoes per square inch on my tent flap, and it was nightmarish to think of what it would be like to try to sleep through a night on such an island without the protection of a tent. How did the men who first explored the Yukon and later chased after its gold ever survive?

The next morning I made my break to freedom as quickly as possible and set off for Tanana. It was only 16 miles downriver, yet this short distance seemed to fill almost a full day of traveling as I futilely hacked and cut at the water, tired and sore and discouraged by my lack of progress. I don't know why that particular morning went so badly, but it did. Perhaps it had something to do with my sense of dispair that each stroke did not carry me a mile—when I faced so many hundreds of miles of river, with so little drop, to reach the Bering Sea.

As I turned the point of Mission Hill and came into view of the long row of cabins and churches and stores that make up Tanana, I knew at once that I would be going no further on the Yukon this year. Ahead, as far as I could see out over the left bank of the river, the land was as flat and unmarked as any I had seen in the Flats. The sight of that flat expanse stretching away to the horizon was the answer to my debate; I knew that I had had enough. To continue beyond Tanana would turn the trip from a pleasure to an endurance contest, and I could see no reason to end my journey miserably.

My last evening meal.

During the next day or two in Tanana, I found several ancillary reasons for my decision: my hand, the cheapness of the air fare to Fairbanks, the fact that the first Eskimo village on the river was much further away than I expected, and a letter from Steve Jacobson saying that he was about to marry his Eskimo girl friend, Anna Nicolai, and he hoped I might reach Fairbanks in time to attend the wedding. (In fact, I was three days late, and Steve and Anna were married without me in the improbable sanctuary of Christmas House, North Pole, Alaska.) But all of these were mere rationalizations for a decision I'd made as soon as I saw the land that lay beyond Tanana. I had "come to the end," and now I was going to stop, after 1,200 miles from the snow-clad peaks of Bennett Lake through the maze of the Flats to the boat-laden shore by the town of Tanana.

One moment comes to mind whenever I think about my brief voyage through the northwest wilderness of Canada and Alaska. It involves one of the men in Weisner's store. He came outside and sat with me on a bench set against the wall of the store, and there we entered into a rambling conversation. He happened to mention that his wife had left him, and then, as he looked out over the river, his eyes far off in distant memory, he said:

"She was always wanting to go Outside, to visit her friends or her relatives. I've been here over 30 years now. There's nothing for me out there. It's all here. I love this country. I see no reason to leave it. Ever."

I'm not sure, but I think I understand what he means. I expect to be back.

There's a race of men that don't fit in,
A race that can't stay still;
So they break the hearts of kith and kin,
And they roam the world at will.
They range the field and they rove the flood,
And they climb the mountain's crest;
Theirs is the curse of the gypsy blood,
And they don't know how to rest.

If they just went straight they might go far;
They are strong and brave and true;
But they're always tired of the things that are,
And they want the strange and new.
They say: "Could I find my proper groove,
What a deep mark I would make!"
So they chop and change, and each fresh move
Is only a fresh mistake.

And each forgets, as he strips and runs
With a brilliant, fitful pace,
It's the steady, quiet, plodding ones
Who win in the lifelong race.
And each forgets that his youth has fled,
Forgets that his prime is past,
Till he stands one day, with a hope that's dead,
In the glare of the truth at last.

He has failed, he has failed; he has missed his chance;
He has just done things by half.
Life's been a jolly good joke on him,
And now is the time to laugh.
Ha, Ha! He is one of the Legion Lost;
He was never meant to win;
He's a rolling stone, and it's bred in the bone;
He's a man who won't fit in.

—Robert Service, "The Men That Don't Fit In"

Happy the man, and happy he alone,
He, who can call today his own;
He who, secure within, can say:
"Tomorrow do thy worst, for I have lived today.
Be fair, or foul, or rain, or shine,
The joys I have possessed, in spite of fate, are mine.
Not Heaven itself upon the past has power;
But what has been, has been, and I have had my hour.
                    —Dryden, trans. of Horace

I know a place where there is no smog and no parking problem
and no population explosion . . . no Cold War and no H-Bombs
and no television commercials . . . no Summit Conferences, no
Foreign Aid, no hidden taxes—no income tax. The climate is the
sort that Florida and California claim (and neither has), the land
is lovely, the people are friendly and hospitable to strangers, the
women are beautiful and amazingly anxious to please—
I could go back, I could—.
                    —Robert A. Heinlein, *Glory Road*

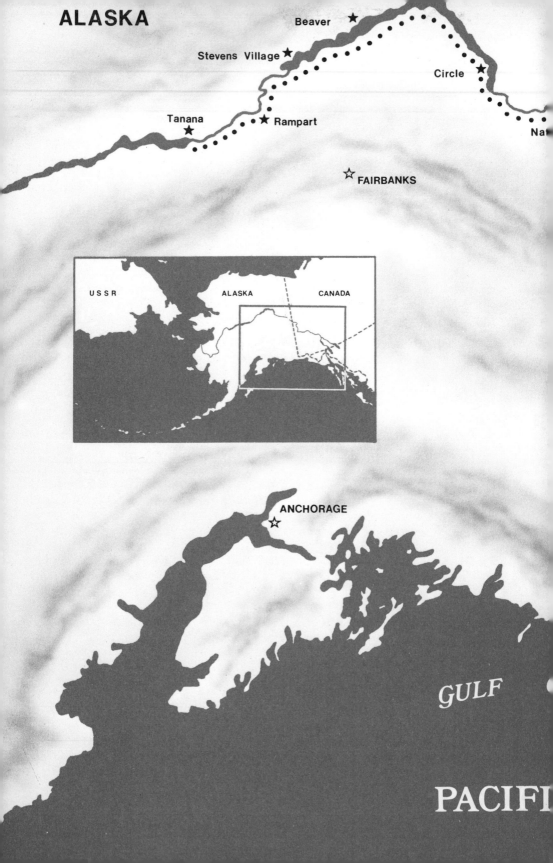